TALES
OF
TUDOR
WOMEN

Marie Sandeford

JOROBY BOOKS

By the same author:
The Second Sister
Long-Lived Ladies and More Tudor Tales

First published in Great Britain in 2003
by Joroby Books, 15 Bridgewater Drive, Great Glen, Leics. LE8 9DX
Reprinted 2012

ISBN-10: 0 9534584 1 5
ISBN-13: 97809534584 1 7

British Library Cataloguing in Publication Data
A catalogue record for this book is available from the
British Library

Printed and bound by CPI Group (UK) Ltd, Croydon, CR20 4YY

Cover illustration: Anne Boleyn

CONTENTS

*Three Tudor Queens and two Kings: Mary, Edward VI, Henry VIII,
his third wife Jane Seymour, and Elizabeth*

INTRODUCTION

'The Monstrous Regiment of Women'

'Women are painted by nature to be weak, frail, impatient, feeble and foolish' and amongst other faults 'unconstant, variable and cruel'. So wrote the 16th-century Scotsman, John Knox, in his *First Blast of the Trumpet against the Monstrous Regiment of Women*. The situation which led to its publication was unprecedented, for both England and Scotland had their first reigning queens.

Most of Knox's venom was directed against England's Queen Mary Tudor, whom he called a Jezebel. He declared that it 'was more than a monster in nature that a woman shall reign and have empire above man' and he meant to blow his trumpet twice more on the matter. But fortunately for Tudor women, this did not happen, because the woman who proved to be the greatest of all the Tudor monarchs, Elizabeth I, succeeded to the English throne soon after his first blast appeared. And in her reign, as in her sister Mary's, if any of her subjects were to seek elsewhere for a monarch, they still had to look to women. For the first time ever, the most serious claimants to the throne were female.

The 'Age of Queens' in England lasted for half a century from 1553-1603, with Mary ruling for five years and Elizabeth from 1558. Mary, the elder daughter of King Henry VIII, was personally a very kind woman, but partly due to her religious persecution of women, history has accorded her the infamous nickname of "Bloody Mary". Yet Elizabeth, who could be very vindictive, especially towards women, was a born survivor and earned for herself the names of "Good Queen Bess" and the "Virgin Queen". Even Knox admitted that she was a genius, although he tried to reason away that she ruled by a particular dispensation of God's mercy, allowing in her what 'law and nature denied to all other women'.

The influence of other women, though, built up from the very outset of the Tudor period in 1485 towards the success of Elizabeth's reign. Her great-grandmother, Lady Margaret Beaufort, set an example for women to assert themselves in what remained very much a man's world. From her, a link, formed through the generations, had a great effect on Elizabeth. Margaret Beaufort was known as "My Lady, the King's Mother" during the reign of the first Tudor monarch, Henry VII. She was close to her son in her astute and intelligent character as well as age, being only thirteen years older. Her prestige and power at his Court were enormous. She particularly encouraged learning, including a higher level of education than was previously usual for girls. Amongst those who studied alongside the eldest of her great-granddaughters, Mary Tudor, was Katherine Parr, who later achieved the somewhat dangerous honour of being the sixth wife of Henry VIII.

Katherine was much admired as a scholarly woman, but probably even more for her tactfulness. Such qualities ensured for her a better fate than her five predecessors, as shown in the old rhyme about Henry's queens - 'divorced, beheaded, died, divorced, beheaded, survived'. The affection which the young Elizabeth felt for Katherine is well recorded. In *this* stepmother, Elizabeth found the kindred spirit she needed to provide positive support for her studies. Thanks to Katherine Parr inspiring the future queen, women were to stay in the ascendant for the rest of the Tudor period.

And this was in spite of their legal status of subservience - not only were wives' property and money deemed to belong to their husbands, but all their possessions too, including clothes and jewels. A London widow called Constance Field even found in 1581 that her husband bequeathed the new mattress on her bed to their maidservant, Rose James! Joan Bastard of Dorset was at least left with her feather bed plus some household utensils, by her late husband, but that was all and only on condition that she did not remarry. The family property of three houses passed to her sons.

Situations sometimes arose in which the control of wives' belongings rebounded on husbands. When two Sussex farmers' wives broke the law in 1561 by wearing black velvet capes, for instance, the spouses of both were fined because farmers were not of high enough rank for their women to be clothed in such finery. A 17th-century chronicle about Sudbury in Derbyshire tells how Margaret Vernon resorted to devious means to find out how her husband planned to bequeath her own inheritance: while a maid kept watch for her, she let herself into his study by unlocking the door with 'a crooked wyer'. One time when she took a supply of pen and ink in with her, she secretly erased her elder son's name from parts of her husband's will so that some property could be left to her younger son.

The name of the maid who acted the crucial role of lookout for Margaret is not recorded. She was probably a trusted friend and companion of her mistress, however, as well as a partner in crime! Although Tudor women from lower and middle social ranks tend to be less well documented than those who were wealthy, the names of some of them and their occupations have become known to posterity through documents such as the wills, letters and household accounts of richer people. Another source of insight comes from church or secular court records, if women happened to be plaintiffs or defendants. The Court-book for Northleach, Gloucestershire, in 1577 referred to a female plaintiff from a village about five miles away as 'Agnes Lawrence of Bourton, foreigner', who successfully obtained the payment of an overdue debt from 'John Groves', inhabitant'. In Essex, the commotion caused by a woman called Dorothy Richmond can easily be imagined. Feeling bored with the Sunday service at Great Holland Church, she jabbed a pin into the buttocks of an unsuspecting woman, Edy Alefounder, and was brought before the county's church courts for her misdemeanour. Pre-marital sex even between betrothed couples was also regarded as an offence - an unmarried woman usually slept with a female relative, who would often be lying in the same bed as the lovers! But the ardour of Elizabeth Jennings and her fiance Richard Shorten of Hatfield Peverel does not appear to have been dampened by the presence of her mother sharing the bed with them.

Surviving parish registers certainly do give many names of Tudor women in their lists of hatches, matches and dispatches. Some parishes favoured more fulsome entries, which reveal graphic details such as the following:

1600, at Chipping, Lancashire. '15 Auguste. Isabell Gregson alias Parker baste daughter of Thomas Parker of Grastonlee ... being by misfortunat chaunce upon a heble [plank bridge] goinge over was drowned ... for want of a good bridge.'

February 1569, at Bobbingworth, Essex. 'George Bourne ... was christened by Mother Wryte, the midwife of the parish and in the presence of ix other honest women ... through great peril and danger.'

A young Peterborough woman called Sarah Lansdune wrote the entries in her church's registers in 1599 when she 'did coppye this Register Book with her own handes'. Women also served in the often demanding office in Tudor times of churchwardens - the Devon village of Kilmington had something of an Elizabethan tradition of them, with Joane Banke in 1560, Elizabeth Grendfeld nine years later, then Elizabeth Norrys the following year, Bryget Dowe in 1574, Agnes Annynge in 1578 and Frances Banckes in 1581.

Against the odds of the social and legal restrictions upon them, a remarkable number of Tudor women adapted in their own way and found a role for themselves, whether this was for good or bad. Some women, such as Bess of Hardwick, made a career of advantageous marriages, but others went to great lengths to marry for love - one girl, Elizabeth Spencer, successfully eloped in a bread basket! Mary Honywood of Kent gained her claim to fame at the other end of life's spectrum. She was one of many Tudor women who lived to a ripe old age, having survived the ordeal of giving birth maybe a dozen times or more. No others accumulated the sheer number of descendants of this great-great-grandmother in her lifetime, though: with her sixteen children, 114 grandchildren, 228 great-grandchildren and nine great-great-grandchildren, she had in total the equivalent of one for every day of the year, plus two.

In Kent is also surely one of the most unusual memorials to a Tudor woman. On the village green at Pembury is a combined horse trough, dog trough and drinking fountain which commemorates Margery Polley, the first of the eighteen Protestant women martyrs from this county in Mary Tudor's reign.

Queens, martyrs, medical women, romantic heroines, businesswomen and craftswomen, were but a part of the very active female contribution to the eventful Tudor period, in addition to the traditional domestic and family roles. The women of Tudor England were indeed far from Knox's description of their gender as weak, frail and feeble.

Almost a century after the 'Age of Queens', another writer, William Wootton, declared that history could not tell of 'so many great women in any one age' as the 16th century. English people seemed to agree more with his view, especially in relation to Queen Elizabeth herself. They continued to keep the date of her accession to the throne, 17th November, as a national holiday for over 200 years after her death. The energy and confidence of her subjects was evident even over her funeral arrangements, when the royal milliner, Dorothy Speckard, earned considerable wealth by supplying the mourning apparel for all the ladies of the Court. Dorothy also charged the cost of her own outfit to the royal accounts!

Memorial to Margery Polley, Pembury, Kent

Dorothy Vernon

CHAPTER 1

The Princess of the Peak

Dorothy Vernon viewed with great pleasure the beauties of each changing season around her home at Haddon Hall in the Derbyshire Peak District. The lovely old house was Dorothy's home for most of her life and still appears much as it was in Tudor times. Various features are named after her, including the little bridge and the door and steps which are all associated with her reputed elopement from Haddon with her cousin, John Manners. There is also a Dorothy Vernon Walk on the highest of the attractive, south-facing garden terraces.

In her own day, Dorothy was very closely connected with well-known historical figures such as the captive Mary Queen of Scots, Mary's custodian the Earl of Shrewsbury and his indomitable wife, Bess of Hardwick. But her fame in modern romance comes from the story of her elopement, which has inspired poems, novels and plays. Haddon Hall itself has provided the setting for numerous film and TV dramas. Ironically, though, the 1920s silent film *Dorothy Vernon of Haddon Hall*, starring Mary Pickford as Dorothy, involved a replica of Haddon being built in Hollywood.

Haddon Hall, Derbyshire

The Vernon family became noted for their great hospitality and the splendour of their banquets and festivities, all of which earned for Dorothy's father, Sir George, the informal title of "the King of the Peak". Dorothy's mother and sister were both called Margaret, but the Haddon household accounts reveal a way of avoiding any potential confusion: Lady Vernon was usually addressed as "my lady" and her daughters as "Mistress Margaret" and   "Mistress Dorothy"! Born in 1545, Dorothy was the younger of the two by five years. The closeness of her immediate family was very much part of her childhood. Then suddenly when she reached her early teens, the world that she knew and loved fell apart. Her mother died in 1558, and added to the trauma of this for such a young girl, her sister married in the same year and left home to live far away on the Isle of Man, and her father remarried.

The household accounts mention Margaret Vernon playing games of 'tables' (backgammon) with her husband-to-be, the handsome Sir Thomas Stanley, second son of the Earl of Derby.   There are also entries in the accounts referring to the negotiations between the two families concerning this arranged marriage. Sir George's new wife was a Derbyshire lady called Maud Longford. She wedded him to please her own family. According to her time-worn epitaph in North Cadbury Church, Somerset, 'her youth was tyed to age far spent' and 'choice of friends brought her to marriage bed'.

Dorothy feared for her own future after seeing her young stepmother's enforced union with the formidable Sir George. She had good reason to regard this as an ominous sign of what might be in store for herself, with her father now in sole charge of deciding upon a husband for her. She knew he would be implacable if his choice were not to her liking! Sir George could indeed behave like a king - a very autocratic king. His mother, yet another Margaret, had received a letter from none other than Henry VIII when she was left a widow with her three year old son, in 1517. King Henry wanted her to marry William Coffin, a Devon knight who was one of his special group of companion servants called the minions. After she wedded Sir William, Lady Vernon probably found that he could conduct himself like his royal master in his occasionally imperious ways and this trait may well have influenced her son. In May 1536, Henry appointed her to attend upon - or rather, inform upon - his second queen, Anne Boleyn, during Anne's imprisonment in the Tower of London shortly before her execution.

Margaret Coffin's next husband was Sir Richard Manners, the uncle of John, her granddaughter Dorothy's future sweetheart. Again, the close circle of the Tudor Court seems to have played a part in bringing about this third marriage. John's mother Eleanor, Countess of Rutland, was a favourite lady-in-waiting, for instance, of all the last four of Henry's wives - Jane Seymour, Anna of Cleves, Catherine Howard and Katherine Parr.

However, differences of religious belief divided the Vernon and Manners families after Henry broke away from the Roman Catholic faith and appointed himself in place of the Pope as head of the English Church. The Vernons of Haddon remained Catholics, like most of the Derbyshire gentry, but the Manners became committed Protestants. Mary Tudor's restoration of Catholicism as the national religion during her brief reign ended with her death in that year of personal upheaval for Dorothy, 1558, and then the Protestant church services were revived by Queen Elizabeth. The Vernons conformed to attending these, but they hardly relished doing so. Although Dorothy was only thirteen, the scene for confrontation with "the King of the Peak" seemed already set if she ever aimed to marry a man whose faith was contrary to that of her father. She and her sister were co-heiresses to the Vernons' extensive property, and several male cousins from within the family were potential suitors. From Sir George's point of view, an alliance between Dorothy and one of these had the advantage of keeping Haddon Hall in the Vernon name.

The story goes that Dorothy and John eloped during the ball in celebration of Margaret's wedding and they rode to Aylestone Church in Leicester, where they were married secretly the next day. Dorothy's extreme youth in 1558 has meant that the usual date for their romantic escapade is given as 1563. But by then, her sister had become the mother of two sons, of whom the first-born died as a baby and the younger boy, Edward Stanley, lived to reach his three score years and ten. Haddon's household accounts no longer exist between 1558 and 1564, and so they can shed no light on when or where Dorothy and John were united. And due to the lack also of any other contemporary historical documents recording these details, many attempts have been made to dismiss the elopement story.

Yet there are hints of this Tudor tale causing a stir at the Elizabethan Court well into the late 16th century. One of Good Queen Bess's maids of honour then was Elizabeth Vernon, a kinswoman of Dorothy's from a Shropshire branch of the family. She and the Earl of Southampton - Shakespeare's patron - fell in love, and rumours flew around wildly that she might elope with him, a way which as one courtier noted was 'hereditary to her name'.

In Derbyshire, the early 17th-century chronicle mentioned in the Introduction, pointed to some kind of discord over Dorothy's marriage. Its author, John Harestaffe, blamed "great Talbott" for 'goodlie landes' passing out of the Vernons' possession. "Great Talbott" was George, Earl of Shrewsbury, the most powerful man in the north Midlands and what was more, his first wife, Lady Gertrude, was John Manners' sister. The Shrewsburys' friendship with Dorothy and John made them very valuable allies, if need be, against "the King of the Peak".

The strong, oral tradition of storytelling in the Peak District itself flourished for centuries and Dorothy's elopement story lingered into the 19th century as part of this. Janetta Manners, Duchess of Rutland, wrote in her book about Haddon Hall in 1890 that she believed the elopement 'may have some historical foundation', but the lengthy passage of time has inevitably brought variations in the contents of the story. The first published version by Allan Cunningham in 1822 referred clearly to the story's survival through the oral tradition but made no mention, for instance, of Margaret's wedding or of any clandestine ceremony for Dorothy. Cunningham described Dorothy escaping through her bedchamber window during a hunting festival at Haddon in the spring of 1563. This accords with the little which is known about Dorothy in her youth more closely than the usual story. Her elopement down the Dorothy Vernon Steps first appeared in *The Love Steps of Dorothy Vernon* by Eliza Meteyard, published in 1860.

Aylestone Church was some sixty miles from Haddon, and sufficiently far away in Tudor times for the tying of a love-knot. It was not necessarily far from Sir George Vernon's disapproval, however. He owned the manor of Aylestone and was patron of its rector, William Heathcot, whose livelihood would have been at risk if he ministered at a secret wedding for Dorothy and John. Maybe Sir George agreed to the match very reluctantly, but would not allow it to take place at Haddon and so Aylestone was chosen instead. Dorothy later inherited this manor and several of her eldest son's children were born there.

An intriguing reference exists to a 'Dorrythie Vernon, chamberer' who served in Katherine, Countess of Huntingdon's household at Ashby-de-la-Zouch Castle, Leicestershire, in 1564. The exact identity of the lady is unknown and since 'Dorothy' was amongst the dozen or so most popular Tudor girls' names, she could have been a namesake from another branch of the Vernon family. Indeed, the tenuous link between the Vernons of Haddon Hall and the Earl of Huntingdon's family came through two women with this Christian name, Lady Dorothy Port and Lady Dorothy Hastings. The first was Maud's mother and the second, her stepsister (Hastings was the Huntingdon family name, and in 1595 this Dorothy became the next Countess).

Like Sir George, both these women were Catholics, a complete contrast in their religion from Countess Katherine and her husband, who were strict Puritans. To devout Catholics, placing the young heiress of Haddon in such a zealous Protestant household was rather hazardous. The Shrewsburys would have been more appropriate hosts if Sir George wished his daughter to serve in a noble household during her education. He was close enough to them to be the godfather of at least one of their children and although Countess Gertrude herself came from a leading Protestant family, she was a gentle, gifted woman free of religious extremes.

By 1565, Dorothy and her father were certainly reconciled. His will is the first document to mention her under her married name. She and John lived at Wiverton in Nottinghamshire during the early part of their marriage, but at the age of only twenty-two she inherited her beloved childhood home much sooner than anticipated. Sir George died in August of that year, providing Lady Maud with a lifetime possession of Haddon Hall amongst other valuable property. As her epitaph relates, though, Maud very swiftly 'pleased herself, who others pleased before' and determinedly 'made her second match by her own choice'! She gave up all her widow's third of the Vernon estates and this was divided between Dorothy and Margaret. Already, Haddon Hall had belonged to Dorothy's ancestors for 400 years. It is still owned by her direct descendants, the Manners family.

Maud has suffered from her stereotyped portrayal in some 19th-century stories and novels as the cruel stepmother, who subjected Dorothy to such indignities as 'three hours of tenter-stitch and an hour to the virginal' starting at 8 a.m. Perhaps the real Maud saw Dorothy as a role model instead and followed her stepdaughter's example by making a happy love-match for herself. She succeeded in her hopes - her second marriage lasted for twenty-nine years 'in joy and comfort great', despite the strong opposition she faced from her own family. They were against the match not only because of the 'wealth and goods great store' which she surrendered but also their deep religious differences from her new spouse, Sir Francis Hastings. He was as Puritan as his eldest brother, the Earl of Huntingdon. Maud and her 'choice' lived for many years in the attractive Elizabethan manor house which still survives near the village church at North Cadbury.

Dorothy enjoyed her role as the Lady of Haddon for the rest of her life. Her first child, George, was born in 1569 and was followed by three more offspring - her daughter, Grace, and sons, Roger and John. George appears to have been the adventurous one, Grace was quiet and modest, and Roger was very studious. All three survived into adulthood, but sadly the youngest, John, was not so robust and died when he was fourteen.

Although Haddon could be very remote during severe winter weather in the Peak District, Dorothy and her husband were kept well-informed for much of the time about the events at Queen Elizabeth's Court. John Manners' brother, Roger, was a member of the royal household and wrote regular letters to his Derbyshire relatives. Other family connections, however, involved royal matters much closer to home.

The Earl of Shrewsbury became the custodian of Mary Queen of Scots for fifteen years of her captivity in England. Bess of Hardwick had been his second Countess for only a year before this daunting task began. A general 'mislike of my Lord's marriage with this wife' had caused a servant called John Hall to resign from the Earl's household, and when Mary was imprisoned at Bess's house, Chatsworth, only two miles from Haddon, in the summer of 1570, a plot to rescue her deeply involved Hall - and Dorothy's own brother-in-law, Thomas Stanley! Fortunately for Dorothy, John and their baby son, a lengthy visit to Wilton House in Wiltshire ensured that they were well away from

Derbyshire at this troubled time. At Wilton they were the guests of their niece - Shrewsbury's eldest daughter, Katherine, Countess of Pembroke. The plot failed before any actual attempt was made to help the Queen of Scots escape, but Thomas Stanley and his accomplices were confined as 'close prisoners' in the Tower of London. Dorothy felt torn between the conflicting emotions of her sympathy for Thomas and loyalty to Lord Shrewsbury. As time passed, though, the good friendship which she and John had long enjoyed with the Earl strengthened even more.

Despite the intrigues and plots surrounding the royal captive, Dorothy and her family sometimes shared social gatherings such as musical entertainments with Mary and the Shrewsburys. Mary may also have given Dorothy a gift of her own needlework - a tapestry of her father, King James V of Scotland, which once hung in Dorothy's bedchamber at Haddon.

Topiary work at Haddon Hall, showing the boar's head crest of Dorothy Vernon's family and the peacock crest of John Manners' family

The Long Gallery and gardens at Haddon Hall gained their present appearance while Dorothy and John lived there. The topiary work includes the family crest of the

Vernons and Manners - a boar's head and a peacock, standing appropriately side by side. In contrast, the Elizabethan house built at Chatsworth by Bess of Hardwick lasted until the late 17th century and its 'great expence' contributed towards the breakdown of her marriage to the Earl of Shrewsbury. The strain of guarding Mary Queen of Scots for so many years also added considerably to the Shrewsburys' acrimonious separation. Increasingly, the Earl turned to Dorothy and John for support, and they proved themselves to be true 'friends in need'. Queen Elizabeth relieved him of his 'charge' as he called the Queen of Scots, in January 1585. When John Manners assisted in escorting Mary away from Shrewsbury's custody, however, he was still mourning for his beloved wife. Dorothy died on 12th June 1584, aged thirty-nine, and was laid to rest near her parents in the Vernon Chapel at Bakewell Church.

Allan Cunningham's story about her elopement mentioned the tradition around Haddon praising Dorothy's 'sunny brown' hair. When the tomb she shares with John and their youngest son was opened during some restoration work on Bakewell Church in 1841, she was found to have lovely auburn hair which was very long. The headdress and veil on her effigy cover most of this outstanding feature, but it enhanced her appearance very much when she was young.

There is an effigy of Lady Maud beside those of Dorothy's parents, even though Maud was buried so far away from Derbyshire. But another local link of hers was yet to influence the Manners family. History repeated itself with the loss of Dorothy when her only daughter, Grace, was about the same age as Dorothy herself had been when her mother died. A family letter to John tells that Grace was comforted by her cousins at Belvoir Castle in Leicestershire, where she was 'very welcome, being bereft of her mother'.

Grace suffered grief as deeply as the young Dorothy in 1558. There was to be no stepmother for Grace, though -

John Manners lived as a widower for the remaining twenty-seven years of his life, a rare occurrence in Elizabethan and early Stuart times. In 1590, Grace married Sir Francis Fortescue of Salden in Buckinghamshire, whose father was the Chancellor of the Exchequer. The match was much approved of by both families and proved to be happy. It produced thirteen offspring.

A description of life at Salden by a visitor there in July 1599 gave the impression of a lively and very busy household run by Grace, who hardly had a minute to herself amid the various comings and goings. The visitor played cards with her and other family members on his first day at Salden, but was unable to speak to her alone. She did not know him, although she had no doubt heard about the adventurous Derbyshire Catholic priest, John Gerard, who was the son of another of Lady Maud's stepsisters, Lady Elizabeth Gerard. His father had taken part in Grace's uncle, Thomas Stanley's plot to free Mary Queen of Scots. John Gerard had arrived at Salden with a priest called Roger Lee, who was a cousin of Grace's husband. Both were disguised as noblemen and were greeted with warmth and kindness by the Fortescues. Perhaps the common ground of coming from the same part of England as Gerard, of recognizing in his voice traces of the local accent familiar to her as a girl, gave Grace some natural rapport with him.

On the second day of his visit, she found that an extra household task required her attention. A small clock needed re-winding, but as she went to deal with this by a bay-window in the dining-room, Gerard approached her. Grace was completely taken aback when this exceptionally tall and well-dressed guest told her his real identity and offered to convert her to the Catholic faith - immediately if she so wished! In his autobiography, Gerard later wrote favourably of her meek and self-effacing demeanour. Here was a woman for whom he thought he could set high spiritual ideals to aim for. While Grace listened to him near her dining-room window, something of what he said

Effigy of Dorothy's daughter, Lady Grace Fortescue, at Mursley Church, Buckinghamshire

clearly struck an answering chord in her. A kind of homecoming began to open up for her to learn more of the religion of her Vernon ancestors, a faith which her relatives on Dorothy's side of the family still followed.

Grace was actively encouraged in her decision to become a Catholic by her husband Francis. He was so well disposed towards the religion that he attended some of Gerard's sermons with Grace and even helped to set the altar for Mass, but he stayed an Anglican himself so as not to displease his father. Queen Elizabeth had refused to set up prisons for shutting away Catholic women "like nuns in a convent", as she stated bluntly, and since Grace was legally subject to Francis, she was less likely than he would be to suffer fines and imprisonment for breaking the law by practising the Catholic faith.

The Fortescues added some Catholic servants to their household, including a personal maid for Grace. These people came to Salden on the recommendation of Gerard and were vital in ensuring that the Protestant servants and visitors knew nothing about the new Catholic chaplain who dwelt secretly in two rooms which Grace set aside at the top of the house. A room adjoining these was used as a chapel, an arrangement which allowed the first chaplain, Anthony Hoskins, to minister to Grace and her children, and the Catholic servants and guests for nine years. John Gerard was certainly proved right in telling Grace that Salden was the best English house he knew of, where a resident priest could stay undiscovered so successfully.

One of Grace's sons, Adrian, later became a priest, as did her cousin, Oliver Manners, who was converted to Catholicism under Gerard's guidance. Another unforeseen consequence of Dorothy's elopement and Grace's clock-winding conversion was that the families of the two Vernon sisters of Haddon Hall were brought together again in their grandchildren's generation: Dorothy's grandson, John Fortescue (Grace's eldest son) married his Catholic cousin, Arabella Stanley, the youngest of Margaret Vernon's granddaughters.

CHAPTER 2

'A Notable Cozener'

'There are cozeners abroad,' wrote Shakespeare in *The Winter's Tale* (Act 4, Scene 4), 'therefore it behoves men to be wary.' Women too needed to keep their wits about them, especially if they were targeted by experienced fraudsters such as Judith Philips, who tried to con her victims out of money and valuables on the pretext that through her, they could meet the Queen of the Fairies.

Only in a world where beliefs in fairies were widespread could she have carried out her particular form of swindling for several years. She was also known as Doll Pope and she 'had wandered the country in the company of divers persons calling themselves Egyptians', or gypsies. That way of life was enough in itself to be regarded as a capital offence after a law against associating with gypsies was passed in 1563. Judith was sentenced to death at Salisbury, but 'afterwards had her pardon'.

She then became the wife of John Philips, a London gun-maker. He forbade her to continue with her 'trade of cozenage'. But she had deserted her first husband because they lived in poverty, and she found that life with her new spouse was beset by a similar lack of income. Judith was later held in London's Newgate Prison, where she confessed in January 1595 that she re-offended twice after her second marriage.

Two episodes in particular give an insight into her unscrupulous methods, which caused her interrogator at Newgate to refer to her as 'a notable cozener'. Sometimes she worked with angels - not the heavenly variety, but gold coins with a devil-slaying figure of St Michael on them. She buried an angel and a silver coin beneath a hollow tree, during a secret nocturnal visit to the garden of a rich farmer she had heard about in the Hampshire village of Up Somborne, near Winchester. Enquiries about him in the local area had furnished her with the knowledge that he was involved in legal proceedings against a neighbour. Judith's next ploy was to put on a performance convincing enough for the farmer and his wife to believe that she was one of the sought-after females with magical powers such as fortune-telling, known as wise or cunning women in Tudor times.

Thatched cottage at Up Somborne, Hampshire

For this purpose, she decided to make her way, apparently casually past the farmhouse the next day. Her timing was perfect, for not only was the front door of the house open, but seated by it was the farmer's wife! Judith halted and looked at the woman very fixedly. After she was challenged by her intended victim for staring, she made an attempt at flattery. The farmer's wife was certainly pleased to learn that good luck showed in her face - more than Judith had seen in a woman for a long time.

Their encounter continued with Judith asking earnestly if perchance there was a hollow, holly tree in the garden, with various weeds growing around it. The farmer's wife replied that there was such a tree. She seemed to be taken in by Judith's performance so far. It was time to progress with this situation an important step further - but would the man of the house be as gullible? There was only one way to find out, so Judith made a request to speak to her main prey himself.

His wife led her inside the farmhouse to meet him. The 'notable cozener' then made the most of her chance, using a mixture of cajolery, flattery and an intense study of his face to overcome any possible scepticism on his part. She said that his forehead revealed his involvement in a legal dispute, but he must not fear, for victory would be his. She also offered, in return for a small fee, to tell the couple where they could find hidden treasure near their home.

The farmer smiled, but would not agree to this without actually seeing any treasure. Therein lay no problem for Judith - she promptly directed him to go to the hollow tree in his garden, where to his amazement, his digging of the earth brought to light one each of gold and silver coins. He was duly impressed. The fact that the conwoman now in his company had put the coins there herself at dead of night clearly did not occur to the farmer or his wife! They did not realize either that when she had identified herself to them as an Englishwoman 'from the Pope', she was bluffing even more, using her then surname of Pope. Instead, they were so caught up in their wish for her to point them towards a valuable horde of coins and maybe even jewels. Despite their enthusiasm, however, the farmer did baulk at paying Judith £14, as well as supplying the expensive items which she declared to be vital in their search. White linen of the highest quality only was good enough for meeting the Fairy Queen, of course, and it must be hung in five different places in the most sizeable chamber of the farmhouse. Each of these places also required a candlestick, on top of an angel of gold. And there needed to be a bridle too, plus a saddle which had two new girths.

When all was ready, Judith went into the garden again

with both the farmer and his wife, where she bade him to go down on his hands and knees. She then attached the bridle and saddle to him, and seating herself side-saddle on his back, she rode him between the house and hollow tree three times. Even after she dismounted, that was not the end of his humiliating treatment by her. The farmer's wife now joined him in being told to lie down flat on her stomach under the tree and to stay there for three hours. Judith said that she would return to them, but in the meantime her place was back in the linen-hung chamber on their behalf, so that she could greet the Queen of the Fairies there.

Judith Philips, the 'notable cozener', thus ensured that she would be undisturbed while she pocketed the angels of gold and packed the linen into a bundle, in preparation for her quick getaway. She put on a white smock and draped a white covering in loose folds over her head, then emerged very briefly into the garden as an ethereal being holding a wand. Her victims thought that the Fairy Queen had favoured them with a rare glimpse of her. Only when Judith failed to come back after the three hours were their suspicions aroused. Lying on the ground under the tree had made them near-frozen by then and the farmer still wore the saddle and bridle! These were removed before he and his wife ventured into the large chamber, where to their horror, they discovered the truth of their plight. Judith and the money and fine linen had vanished.

The couple were too shocked and embarrassed at first, too deterred perhaps by the fear of facing disbelief or ridicule over her deception of them, to try pursuing her. Fortunately for them, the husband rallied sufficiently to ride the short distance to Winchester and confide in his kinsman there about what had happened. Judith soon suffered a great shock herself, when her male victim and his relative raised hue and cry in chase of her. She was caught and imprisoned!

Her 'subtill practises' towards a widow from London were denounced as 'unwomanly' by a contemporary commentator. The incident took place after Judith married John Philips, so he was put in Newgate with her during the investigations. Unlike her, though, he attracted sympathy both from the interrogator and the widow, a Mrs Mascall, as he 'could say nothing but by the report of his wife'. Judith was blamed by one of her accomplices for suggesting their plot to defraud Mrs Mascall 'of her money and plate'. This man, Peters, had not wished to cozen the widow but to marry her. According to Judith's version of events, he and his associate, Vaughan, had sought her assistance to try and gain this lady's favour towards Peters. Vaughan made up a letter, pretending that it was from a close friend of Mrs Mascall's called Mr Grace. Judith Philips was highly recommended in it as someone 'who could do her great good'. The recipient later admitted that when Judith visited her with this letter, she 'put the same in her bosom' and found 'she had no power to deny Philip's wife anything'.

Judith's two partners in crime passed on to her much information about Mrs Mascall, so that 'she might seem to be a wise woman' to her unsuspecting victim. She was warmly welcomed, even into the widow's chamber, where she went through the usual charade of appearing to be able to tell fortunes. She 'read' Mrs Mascall's palm before reeling off the names of the suitors she had been given by Peters and Vaughan. She next acted upon some instructions from Peters, by enquiring about unexplained lights and noises in the house, which troubled Mrs Mascall at night. Judith was asked how she knew of these. "I know it well," she replied, "and the cause too, for there is money hid in your house."

As before with the Hampshire farmer, Judith offered to help in locating a fictitious store of money and attracted very eager agreement to the idea! The elated widow was now much under the illusion that her visitor did indeed have great skill as a wise woman, and she began to speak more openly about her suitors. Afterwards, she denied Judith's assertion that she attempted to find out who her next husband would be - or that she expressed a strange-sounding wish to know first 'when the world should turn', even before she would consent to marry her favourite suitor, a rich old gentleman.

Whatever was said, the conwoman seemingly could not give a satisfactory answer to her victim straightaway, so she used delaying tactics to help her continue with this latest deceit. She promised 'to get the money hid in the house' for Mrs Mascall on her next visit. True to form, Judith then added that first she must have the lady's own gold - not for conveying away, but to leave wherever Mrs Mascall chose inside the house, and within two days, the hidden gold should appear in that appointed place! Mrs Mascall duly obliged by bringing out various gold pieces, including a chain, seven rings and a whistle. At Judith's request, these were put into a purse and then passed to her, using the right hand. The purse was next wrapped by Judith in yarn. But little did Mrs Mascall know that two stones had already been 'wound up in like yarn' and these were handed to her, while Judith kept the gold loot.

The widow was unaware too of further attempts to trick her. She was told to put the yarn and its contents away in the place intended for the hidden gold treasure and not to undo the yarn for another three days. She had to give Judith a turkey and a capon, supposedly for the Fairy Queen, and also to say 'certain prayers in sundry places of her house'. The reality was more colourful that this brief account in Judith's confession and involved rituals such as cutting the victim's pubic hair, plying her with alcohol and marrying her to Peters while she was too drunk to realize.

Judith claimed Mrs Mascall's seven rings for herself and shared out the remaining gold pieces three ways with Peters and Vaughan. As for the meat, she carried the turkey's head and one of its legs in a basket to the victim's house the next day. Her aim this time was to make off with valuable utensils. She began by saying that the leg must be placed under Mrs Mascall's bed and the head elsewhere.

The lady listened attentively, but could now see through Judith's lies - and not only because she had discovered the two stones in the yarn handed to her the previous day! The 'notable cozener' had not reckoned on this turn of events, and an unpleasant surprise awaited her. Mrs Mascall had her arrested.

St Valentine's Day in 1595 was no romantic occasion for the deceitful Judith Philips. She was sentenced to the brutal punishment of being publicly whipped through the City of London.

THE

Brideling, Sadling and Ryding, of

a rich Churle in Hampſhire, by the ſubtill practiſe of one
Iudeth Philips, a profeſſed cunning woman, or
Fortune teller.

VVith a true diſcourſe of her vnwomanly vſing of a Trype wife, a widow,
lately dwelling on the back ſide of S. Nicholas ſhambles in London, whom ſhe with her conferates, likewiſe coſoned:

For which fact, ſhee was at the Seſſions houſe without New-gate arraigned,
where ſhe confeſſed the ſame, and had iudgement for her offence,
to be whipped through the Citie, the 14. of February, 1594.

Printed at London by T. G. and are to be ſolde by
William Barley, at his ſhop in New-gate
Market, neare Chriſt-Church. 1595.

Judith Philips, as shown in 'The Brideling, Sadling and Ryding of a rich Churle in Hampshire', published in 1595. (This item is reproduced by permission of The Huntington Library, San Marino, California)

CHAPTER 3

The 'Knot of Secret Might'

One day in December 1560, Elizabeth I decided to leave the cares of state behind for a short while, by going from Whitehall Palace to stay at Greenwich Palace for a few days' hunting at nearby Eltham. She had recently celebrated the second anniversary of her accession to the throne and felt able to relax, especially as her grip on power seemed to be strengthening each day. Her rival, Mary Queen of Scots, had already been the queen consort of France for over a year and the death of Mary's mother, Mary of Guise, six months before had brought to an end the latter's rule as the regent in Scotland for a more friendly and pro-English regime.

Elizabeth ordered her young maids of honour to prepare to accompany her the following morning. But before daylight, two of them came to her in a state of some distress, declaring that they felt too unwell to go to Greenwich. The Queen looked with sympathy at the older girl, Lady Jane Seymour, a favourite of hers and the namesake and niece of her father Henry VIII's beloved third wife. With a sigh of regret, she readily gave Jane permission to remain at Whitehall. The poor soul was often ailing, though not with the complaint which afflicted the other girl and increasingly troubled Elizabeth herself - *toothache!*

The tiny figure of Elizabeth's cousin, Lady Catherine Grey, stood before her with a visibly swollen cheek and a kerchief tied round her face in the hope of easing the pain. Despite Catherine's predicament, however, Elizabeth frowned in her habitual way at this attractive twenty year old, whom many people both in England and abroad regarded as the heiress to her throne. Elizabeth had no intention of naming Lady Catherine or anyone else as her successor, but the royal pangs of jealousy stirred again

Lady Catherine Grey

when she allowed her cousin to stay behind too. She did not share the feelings which had made Jane Seymour and Catherine Grey become the best of friends. And she certainly did not support the widespread sympathy amongst her subjects towards Catherine as the younger sister of Lady Jane Grey, the tragic nine-days' Queen of England, who was beheaded at the tender age of sixteen. The Grey sisters were granddaughters of King Henry's favourite sister Mary and his will had placed them in the line of succession immediately after Elizabeth. Catherine had also inherited her beauty from her Tudor grandmother, as well as her claim to the throne.

Soon after Elizabeth left for Greenwich, the two friends made an instant recovery and set off on a journey of their own. They had already sent their servants on various errands, so they were able to slip away unnoticed from the palace, avoiding the main watergate by going through the orchard and down a flight of steps, which led from there to the river Thames. The water was at low tide and they squelched along the pebbly, muddy river bank, overjoyed to have outwitted their formidable Queen. After a few hundred yards, they reached the river stairs of their destination - the Westminster town house of Jane Seymour's brother and Catherine's betrothed, Edward, Earl of Hertford.

When they entered Hertford House and were greeted by the handsome, but nervous young Earl, Catherine may have reflected that her wedding to him would have been a splendid occasion if Queen Mary Tudor had lived long enough to sanction their marriage. She had approved of the romance between Catherine and Edward which began in 1554, but they both came from renowned Protestant families and felt constrained to tread warily amid the religious persecutions of the Catholic Mary's reign. They had hoped to marry when Edward came of age around 1559 and could take full control of his Seymour inheritance. By then, however, Elizabeth was Queen and she had a great aversion to marriage!

This strong trait in Elizabeth combined with an aura of majesty which the young couple found intimidating. As Catherine was a lady of royal blood, they needed the monarch's permission for her to marry. They felt afraid of trying to obtain this, but even so, several attempted approaches were made. Unfortunately, these foundered at a time when, ironically, public attention was scandalized by Elizabeth's own close companionship with Catherine's married brother-in-law, Lord Robert Dudley, and the mystery surrounding his wife Amy's sudden death in September 1560. Mary Tudor's husband, King Philip of Spain, was rejected as a suitor by Elizabeth and he sought to maintain some influence in England instead by intriguing to abduct Catherine, wed her to a Spanish prince and then uphold her claim to the throne against that of Mary Queen of Scots.

Finally, the fear of being kidnapped by Spaniards, and despair over any favourable response from Elizabeth after six long years of courtship by Edward, caused Catherine to agree to a secret wedding. "I am well content," she told him, "be the consequences what they may." Their betrothal took place in his sister Jane's private sitting-room at Whitehall. Catherine's betrothal ring was gold with a pointed diamond, and she wore this soon after she arrived at Hertford House on that December morning. Shortly she would wear her wedding ring, which was one of the 'posy' rings so popular then. These opened into several sections and revealed a personal inscription inside. The Latin words in Catherine's ring translated as follows:

'As circles five by art compressed show but one ring to sight,
So trust uniteth faithful minds with knot of secret might
Whose force to break but greedy death no wight possesseth power,
As time and sequels well shall prove; my ring can say no more.'

Queen Mary had inadvertently eased Catherine's decision, by repealing the law which made the offence one of treason for any subject to marry a member of the royal family without the monarch's consent. The various preparations for tying the 'knot of secret might' included a goodly array of food and wine in the Earl of Hertford's bedchamber, but so far one vital ingredient was still missing. The absence of the clergyman to conduct the ceremony meant a half-hour delay while Jane determinedly went in search of another.

The only hint of what happened between the lovers while they waited completely alone in the bedchamber, came from Catherine herself when she later said that they talked in ways appropriate to people about to be married. Jane Seymour had already helped her best friend's romance with her brother in many ways, such as carrying messages and arranging clandestine meetings between them. She brought back a red-haired, middle-aged minister with her, and Catherine and Edward at last exchanged their wedding vows. No-one thought to ask the man's name, not even the resourceful Jane when she accompanied him down to the main door of Hertford House and paid him £10. She subsequently returned to the bedchamber, but was soon downstairs again, in the parlour, where she at least could have a break from the morning's exertions while the newly-weds consummated their union.

Until now, neither Catherine nor her husband had ever undressed from their elaborate Tudor costume without assistance. But in the necessary absence of their servants, they somehow managed to divest themselves of layers of winter clothing - quite an achievement in itself. Their time together was all too short, however - only about an hour and a half, before circumstances dictated that they struggled back into their clothes and Catherine returned with Jane to Whitehall. If either girl were missing from the midday meal there, awkward questions might be asked by Elizabeth's old governess, Kat Ashley, who was in charge of the Court while the Queen was away.

The tide had risen and a passing boat was hailed for the

journey back by river. A few days later, Edward presented Catherine with a deed which acknowledged her as his wife and settled Seymour lands worth £1,000 a year on her if she became widowed. This document was sufficient proof of their marriage, for English law at the time recognized private weddings which took place elsewhere than in church, and without banns, as long as the nuptial ceremony was confirmed with such an important settlement as dower income.

Catherine's love-match remained a secret until her impending motherhood could no longer be disguised during the next summer's royal progress through Essex and Suffolk. Sadly for Catherine, she was very much alone by then, for her husband was abroad on the Queen's service and their only witness, Jane, died of consumption the previous March. As a further complication, Elizabeth fell into 'a great misliking' with Catherine. Her first marriage to Lord Henry Herbert had been annulled, unconsummated, as a result of her sister Jane Grey's execution. Now he was endeavouring to remarry her and understandably, Catherine would have none of him!

The Queen and Court were staying at Ipswich for a few days, when Catherine's heart sank at an unfortunate discovery - the vital deed of gift given to her by Edward was nowhere to be found. With all the moving about on the progress, it had become lost or possibly stolen. Nor was Elizabeth in any mood to be conciliatory if Catherine sought mercy by confessing about her marriage and pregnancy. The royal temper was even more likely to erupt than usual because of Elizabeth's anger over married clergy, and also the anticipated return of the widowed Mary Queen of Scots from France to her northern realm.

After searching desperately for the deed, Catherine confided her secret to an old family friend of the Greys, Bess of Hardwick. She hoped that Bess would help by interceding on her behalf with the Queen, but she received such short shrift that it added further trauma. Towards midnight on 9th August 1561, she suddenly appeared in

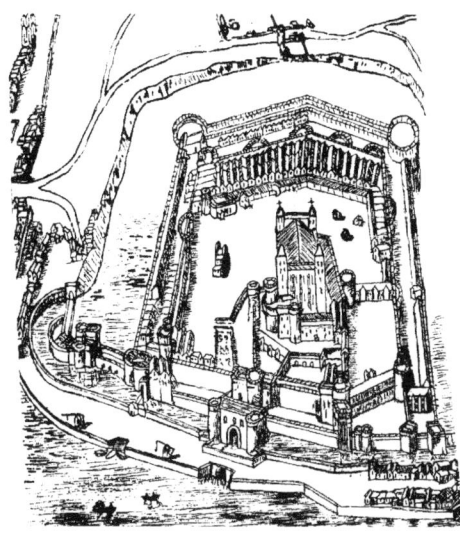

Bird's eye view of the Tower of London in the 16th century

her nightgown at the bedside of another old family connection, Robert Dudley, and knelt down, sobbing, as she told him her story.   Elizabeth was asleep in the adjoining bedchamber and could have burst in at any minute on the sight of her favourite with a young, pregnant woman by his bed! If the Queen had done so, both of them would have been in trouble, but in the morning Catherine took the full brunt of her fury after Robert Dudley told Elizabeth of her cousin's plight.

Catherine was later destined to revisit under house arrest, a very 'sorrowful woman for the Queen's displeasure', three of the stopping-places on that progress - Pirgo, Ingatestone Hall and Gosfield Hall in Essex. But in the meantime, Elizabeth sent Catherine straightaway to the dreaded Tower of London and imprisonment in the very same part where she herself had been held captive briefly in 1554, the Bell Tower. Edward, Earl of Hertford, was also a prisoner in the Tower shortly before Catherine gave birth to their baby, a healthy son who was named after him.

Elizabeth refused to accept that the 'knot of secret might' was a love-match and never part of any plot to seize her throne. Even her chief minister, Sir William Cecil, admitted that he was not 'above suspicion'. He told Elizabeth that her intense anger concerning Catherine's marriage was an over-reaction. Many other loyal subjects, rich and poor, also voiced their criticism of the Queen over this matter. But she went against the climate of dissent all too easily. Her royal officials failed to find either the clergyman or the missing deed of gift, and with the witness, Jane Seymour, being dead, Elizabeth wasted little time in having the marriage invalidated.

Feelings of antipathy between Catherine and Elizabeth may have begun amid the bitter friction which haunted the latter's relationship with her sister, Queen Mary. Elizabeth's oft-quoted comment that her own accession to the throne was 'marvellous in our eyes' expressed an opinion probably not shared by Catherine. A letter which she wrote to her husband in the Tower clearly did show the affection between them, however:

'No small joy is it to me, my dear lord, the comfortable understanding of your maintained health. I crave of God to let you sustain, as I doubt not but He will ... Though of late I have not been well, yet now, I thank God, pretty well, and long to be merry with you as you do to be with me ... I have good leisure so to do when I call to mind what a husband I have of you and my great hard fate to miss the viewing of so good a one ...'

Despite Elizabeth's orders that the couple were to be kept apart, they did enjoy the company of each other and their son, and also Catherine's large menagerie of pet dogs and monkeys. And during their two-year captivity in the Tower, Catherine came closest to becoming Queen herself. For when Elizabeth almost died of smallpox in October 1562, the right of Catherine, who was English-born, Protestant and above all, the mother of a son, was considered markedly stronger than that of the only other serious claimant, Mary Queen of Scots. But the promise of glory faded for her, Elizabeth recovered and soon afterwards, Catherine again proved that she was not a 'barren stock' like her Sovereign by providing her first-born, Edward, with a baby brother called Thomas. Other members of the gifted Tudor dynasty failed disastrously in producing healthy male offspring, but both of Catherine's sons survived well into adulthood.

An outbreak of plague in August 1563 prompted Elizabeth to move her two prisoners with their children, whom she referred to as 'their brats', from the Tower to more comfortable but separate custody in country houses near London. Appeals were made by various sympathizers for the couple to be re-united, but some infuriated Elizabeth more by renewed attempts to assert Catherine's claim to the throne.

Eventually, the melancholy of their imprisonment and enforced parting began to take its toll on the slightly-built Catherine's health. Some words written to her in a moving, tear-stained letter from her sister, Lady Jane, on the eve of her execution became strong in their meaning: 'Trust not that the tenderness of your age shall lengthen your life, for as soon as God will goeth the young as the old.' In January 1568, at the age of twenty-seven, Catherine died of consumption at Cockfield Hall in Suffolk. Her last words, "Lord, into thy hands I commend my spirit," were the same as those uttered by Jane Grey on the scaffold almost fourteen years earlier. Catherine even closed her eyes with her own hands just before she died. A devoted pet spaniel kept vigil beside her first burial place in Yoxford Church nearby, and soon pined away.

Her betrothal and wedding rings, and a mourning ring engraved, 'While I lyve, yours', which the Earl of Hertford had sent to her before their removal from the Tower, were all returned to him in accordance with her dying wishes. He was then a prisoner at Althorp House in Northamptonshire, the ancestral home and burial place of their descendant, Princess Diana. His devotion to

Catherine continued during the fifty-three years he outlived her. In 1591 Elizabeth attended a joyously elaborate four-day entertainment at the Seymours' home at Elvetham, Hampshire, during her summer progress. This provided a chance for belated forgiveness concerning the 'knot of secret might' over thirty years before.

The Queen had eventually allowed Lord Hertford's second marriage - to another of her maids of honour, Frances Howard, whose brother led the victory over the Spanish Armada. Frances was affectionately nicknamed "Goode Francke" by Elizabeth and knew that the ageing monarch's vanity must be over-indulged with exaggerated compliments and adulation. Her Majesty's dark and fierce eyes were therefore praised as 'blessed starres', while she stayed at Elvetham. And no way could her increasingly sharp features such as her hooked nose be so described - instead, her appearance gave 'joys exceeding measure' and girls dressed as classical nymphs sang ditties such as, "'Tis fair Elizabeth's matchless grace, who with her beams does bless this place."

In order to gratify Elizabeth's well-known liking for eating sweetmeats, which had caused her remaining teeth to blacken, a prodigious collection of sugar-work creatures, castles and coats-of-arms were served before her. A new withdrawing room resembling a forest bower was also built specially for her, and Frances ensured that it was carpeted with rushes and fragrant herbs to soothe the Queen's acute sense of smell. Frances and her women worked hard too in making costumes for all the various participants in the entertainment, and they sewed sails for the tree-pole masts of an imaginary ship used in the water pageants. Elizabeth enjoyed watching the novelty of history's first-ever game of lawn tennis, but particularly on the final morning did Frances realize how well she had arranged the entertainment: fairies danced then round a crowned silver pole on the tennis lawn and sang yet more profuse praises about Elizabeth, "the fairest Queen that ever trod upon this greene", who ordered a repeat performance!

Four years later, Elizabeth tried to reassure Frances of the 'continuance of our former grace' when the Earl of Hertford sought openly to establish the validity of his youthful marriage to Lady Catherine and was again imprisoned in the Tower. The Queen's genuine friendship was crucial in obtaining his release on payment of a heavy fine. On 24th June 1598, a book in commemoration of Frances was entered in the Registers of the Stationers' Company of London: *Celestial Effigies of the Goddesses and Muses deploringe the death of the right honourable and vertuous Ladie, the Lady Ffraunces, late wife unto the right honourable Edward Seymour, Viscount Beauchamp and Earle of Hertford.* Perhaps appropriately, it was published by a woman, Joan Broome, who had taken over her late husband's printing and publishing business.

Lady Catherine Grey's succession rights passed to her sons, but Elizabeth went on refusing to designate her heir. On her death-bed, she declared that she wanted "no rascal's son" as England's next monarch and this has been misinterpreted as revealing her unabated wrath against Catherine. She was making a metaphorical jibe, though, at Catherine's husband, who was well-known for his deep attachment to the Forest of Savernake he owned in Wiltshire. A 'rascal' then meant an inferior kind of deer, and Elizabeth was pointing out that Catherine's sons were not fully royal-blooded compared with Mary Queen of Scots' son, King James.

Not until three years after Elizabeth's death and forty-six years after the 'knot of secret might' did the minister who had performed the ceremony come forward and place its validity beyond doubt. Catherine and her "good Ned", as she sometimes affectionately called the Earl of Hertford, have their lasting memorial in Salisbury Cathedral's 'Golden Tomb', where part of the Latin epitaph to them translates: ' ... after having experienced alternate changes of fortune, here at last they rest together in the same concord in which they lived.'

Effigies of Lady Catherine and Edward, Earl of Hertford, on their tomb in Salisbury Cathedral

CHAPTER 4

Mrs Minister

What's in a name? An Elizabethan vicar's wife called Mrs Agnes Worship was fortunate, perhaps, that a brass inscription in Croft Church, Lincolnshire, extols her as 'a woman machles both for wisdom and godlynes'. With her name being so appropriate to her role in life, she had something of a higher standard to live up than many women of the Tudor period. No less easy, however, was the day-to-day existence of other ministers' wives with names like Mrs Freake, Mrs Hussey, Mrs Bastard and Mrs Prick in the early generations of married clergy. Not only did these wives face the subservient status of all married women, but this was compounded by the low position of women within the English Church and a general, public prejudice against the marriage of church ministers.

The hostess of a Dover inn, nevertheless, accused all married clergy of clothing and feeding their wives "finely, as if they were ladies of the land". Thomas Bastard, a Dorset vicar, certainly admitted marrying his second wife for her wealth in his middle age, but the first Mrs Bastard was a love-match in his youth and the third was expected to provide comfort in old age (if only each wife's views about her situation had been recorded!).

Elizabeth Massey, the minister's wife in the Tower of London, *did* try to express her opinions concerning one of the guards there and his Catholic sympathies, but she was threatened and assaulted by him for her efforts. The Duke of Norfolk's laundress recruited Mrs Massey to carry secret letters to and from him during his imprisonment in the Tower in 1571 - a potentially lucrative way of supplementing her family's income. She received and delivered the letters via his servant, William Sharpe, and also passed on a silver cross which was a love-token for Sharpe himself from his wife-to-be, Ellen Dyer.

Another way of conveying the secret missives was done by an unnamed woman of Tower Hill and the jailer's maid, Mary Craborne. Elizabeth Massey appears to have raised no objections to this. She did so, however, about a guard called Jervys using his seven year old daughter to take nosegays to the Duke, and the child then being rewarded with gold and silver coins. The minister's wife took exception to such goings-on because she saw and overheard Jervys wishing Catholic prisoners well. When she also overheard him exchanging 'many evil words' with her husband - amongst these that she should be 'put away' - she accused him of being a traitor. Shortly afterwards, he attacked her when she was on her way to report him to the Lieutenant of the Tower.

Being 'ladies of the land' was something that even archbishops' wives could not aspire to, because they were not recognized as sharing their husbands' noble rank - a fact which is well illustrated on the tomb of Archbishop Sandys in Southwell Minster, Nottinghamshire. His second wife, Cecily is relegated to being depicted on an engraving on the front panel, instead of lying in effigy beside him. She is shown at prayer, with their six sons and two daughters behind her - the one concession to her is that she is kneeling on a cushion, but the offspring are not! Her own monument is at Woodham Ferrers, Essex, the home of her predecessor as Mrs Sandys.

The law allowing clergy to marry was still in its infancy when Queen Mary repealed it early in her reign. Few people expected then that there would be a gap of over fifty years before it was restored, or that her Protestant sister Elizabeth would add to the insecurity of ministers' wives with incidents such as her well-known bluntness towards Margaret Parker, the Archbishop of Canterbury's wife: "Madam, I may not call you. Mistress, I am ashamed to call you, so as I know not what to call you ..." Queen Elizabeth's abhorrence of marriage for her clergy was for different reasons from Mary's Catholicism, but it may have been motivated by a genuine religious feeling and also her sheer sense of oneness with her realm of England.

Elizabeth's written, private devotions reveal her greater depth of faith in God than history has often accorded her. She prayed in thanksgiving for her peaceful accession to rule her people and 'nourish' the English Church. She was the Supreme Governor over spiritual as well as secular matters and she appointed all the bishops and archbishops. Much store was set by her on their authority to run a well-ordered national Church, and in her estimation the wedded state of most of them was an extra burden of responsibility which could affect their work. The Virgin Queen observed for herself in 1561 the increased squalor and noise caused by clergymen's wives and children in cathedral and college closes, so she issued at edict which banned them from living in these study-filled surroundings, or else the husbands risked losing their chances of promotion.

As with other groups of Tudor women, some 'Mrs Ministers' sought to overcome adversity in individual ways. Margaret Colfe, the vicar of Lewisham's wife, probably endeared herself to the parishioners there, for instance, because of her medical skills. As her memorial in St Mary's Church, Lewisham, records, she was 'above forty years, willing nurse, midwife, surgeon and in part, physician to both rich and poor without expecting reward ...' In Yorkshire, another Margaret once secretly owned the land where the famous cricket ground at Headingley now stands. This was amongst the property forfeited to the Crown when her husband, Thomas Cranmer, Archbishop of Canterbury, was burnt at the stake in Mary's reign. He had most likely intended to bequeath to his German-born wife the valuable Kirkstall Abbey estate and its extensive lands in the nowadays built-up, surrounding suburbs of Leeds, including Headingley. But Mrs Cranmer gained it instead by obtaining the lease from her husband's former publisher, to whom Queen Mary had granted this.

Insight into the lives of some clergymen's wives emerged when their husbands came more into the

Kirkstall Abbey, Leeds

limelight as bishops. Mrs Cecily Freake was one wife who made her presence known by determinedly refusing to be inferior to her husband Edmund, the Bishop of Norwich. She appointed herself to be a kind of commander-in-chief and perhaps because he was a former monk, he submitted to such dominance. He even said tearfully in 1578 that if he disobeyed her, she made him "weary of his life". Her servants addressed her as "Mrs Bishop" and she vetted everyone who came to see her husband. Woe betide any visitors who brought no gift with them, for she treated them to a withering look, which one servant compared to the ugly, devilish gargoyle known as the Lincoln Imp in Lincoln Cathedral! Elizabethan bishops' palaces were still run in the same way as in the old times, when England was Catholic. In theory, therefore, bishops' wives wielded no domestic power. In practice, however, Mrs Freake caused the bishop to dismiss the steward of the forty-strong Norwich Palace household because she thought the man was too religious. She was also implicated in the dismissal of the chancellor of the diocese, but this led to tales of her domineering character spreading far beyond Norfolk and earned her the censure of the Queen's Privy Council.

Royal anger was directed too at the neighbouring diocese of Ely, partly due to a wife at work in one of the more traditional tasks of the period. The widow of William Turner - Dean of Wells in Somerset and author of one of the first English botanical books, *Turner's Herball* - became Mrs Jane Cox by her second marriage to the elderly widower, Bishop Cox of Ely. Her management of his dairy involved her charging high prices for the episcopal butter and cheese, and this increased Elizabeth's annoyance against him for remarrying. The wives' attempts at money-making were usually for 'necessarie thinges for the sustentation of an honest famylie', as one clergyman put it. Unfortunately their schemes for survival against a precarious and possibly poor background rebounded on some women, as in the cases of Elizabeth Massey and Jane Cox. And amid the prejudice against them, several wives gained a reputation for being avaricious. One of these was Mary Cotton, the Bishop of Exeter's wife, who is said to have accepted bribes in order to speak to him on behalf of petitioners who sought his favour. But as her husband pointed out, their income from his bishopric was low.

Mrs Marion Harrison, wife of the rector of Radwinter in Essex, also found that her husband William wrote of their poverty - in this instance, in his book *A Description of England,* first published in 1577. Over a quarter of their annual income of £40 went on the monthly brewing of the household beer which she and her maids had to do. He detailed the procedure involved 'as she hath oft informed me' - very labour-intensive indeed to produce 200 gallons each time for £1 including costs such as all the ingredients, servants' pay and wear and tear of the equipment needed! The Harrisons' income was increased for several years when he took on an extra position as vicar of the nearby village of Wimbish. But here, Marion fell foul of a woman called Margery Staunton who tended to pester her neighbours with various demands and then utter words of malice against them if they refused. Marion did say "no" to one such request and turned Margery away. Soon after this incident, the Harrisons' young son fell ill. In 1579, Margery Staunton was accused and tried at Chelmsford on several charges of witchcraft, but was not executed because no actual deaths could be proved against her.

William Harrison bore in mind the vulnerability of ministers' wives and the prevailing popular view of them as 'the causes of our woe', when he made his will. He took care to acknowledge Marion as his 'true and lawful wife', and he appointed her and their son as executors. Her share of the bequests was a quarter and half of another quarter of all his goods. Although she died later in the same year as her husband, 1593, and so had little time to benefit from his provision for her, Marion had never had to fear that she would be left without financial support as a widow. Sadly, this was the experience of some of the other women, but William Harrison wrote in defence of clergymen's right to 'leave their substances to their wives and children'.

Church properties such as vicarages, rectories and bishops' palaces were only home for clerical families during the husbands' lifetime, so new widows who were unprovided for faced becoming homeless as well as destitute. In 1574 Mrs Jones, the Bishop of Llandaff's widow, asked permission from the Privy Council to remain in the episcopal palace at Mathern, near Chepstow, until a new bishop was appointed. The blind woman, Elizabeth Best, widow of the Bishop of Carlisle, and Mawde Bentham, the Bishop of Lichfield and Coventry's widow, had no such option to keep a roof over their heads. Mawde even lost some of her furniture in compulsory payment of her husband's debts. Like Cecily Sandys, she was one of the English Protestants who went into exile and married abroad during Mary Tudor's reign, and she and her children are also commemorated on the front panel of her husband's table tomb. But a significant difference is that Thomas Bentham is depicted kneeling there too with his family, having shared their poverty in life. The engraved representation of him alone on top of the tomb is hardly discernible in its very dark corner in the north tower room at Eccleshall Church, Staffordshire.

Mawde Bentham with her husband and children, Eccleshall Church, Staffordshire

Elizabeth Scory's life mirrored even more the ups and downs of being a Tudor clergyman's spouse. She was renounced as his wife when her husband conformed to the Catholic faith under Queen Mary - though fortunately not given up in the extreme way of one of her contemporaries, Mrs Chekyns of London, whose parson husband apparently sold her to a butcher! Mrs Scory was soon reinstated when her husband reverted to Protestantism and she accompanied him into exile. When they returned to England at the start of Elizabeth's reign, he was appointed Bishop of Hereford. He ensured that his wife had a comfortable income from the church at Bromyard in Herefordshire, but his arrangements for their son, Sylvanus, led to an ugly scene in 1585. Elizabeth Scory was ejected from the very room where her husband lay dying at Whitbourne, near Worcester, by her own son when he arrived with armed retainers to claim his inheritance.

A brass memorial of 1581 in the chancel of Heston Church, Middlesex, is a reminder of a potential hazard for all mothers, whatever their social rank, during an age of high rates of infant mortality and deaths in childbirth. It depicts a minister's wife called Constance Bownell in bed and her dead child on the coverlet. Also in the 1580s, the young, pregnant wife of a Sussex clergyman called Dr Becon nearly lost her life after the premature birth of a son, brought on by stress and trauma when her husband was dismissed from his position as chancellor of a Midlands diocese and then 'dispossessed of house, office and money'. Mrs Becon found herself riding over a hundred miles to try and intercede on his behalf, but she suffered discourtesy and abuse from his former colleague, William Overton, Bishop of Lichfield and Coventry, and Overton's first wife, Margaret. What appears to have been particularly galling to the Becons was this bishop's ingratitude towards Mrs Becon, who had been partly instrumental in obtaining his bishopric for him. He had once promised her that he would seek to do the Becons good if she could persuade her husband to help his 'advauncement of living', but he later quarrelled with Becon, who had 'left all' to become his chancellor.

Bishop Overton and his two wives at Eccleshall

Perhaps the Overtons had been mindful of family pressure in their zeal for him to become a bishop. Margaret Overton was the eldest of the five daughters of Bishop Barlow of Chichester and his wife, Agatha, who wished all of them to marry bishops. Margaret was the first to achieve this, but eventually her sisters Ann, Elizabeth, Anthonina and Frances also became bishops' wives. The latter's first marriage was to Matthew Parker, the Archbishop of Canterbury's son, and her second husband was surnamed Matthew! He was appointed Bishop of Worcester in 1594, and later moved north to be the Bishop of Durham and subsequently, the Archbishop of York. An income which he established for Frances from northern property had her brother John and one of her bishop brothers-in-law as trustees.

Despite occurrences when all was clearly not such mutual help and harmony between or even within the Protestant clerical families, the old principle of safety in numbers inevitably brought them together through their committed religious beliefs and the outside hostility against them. Other ministers' wives from a clerical background themselves included Martha, the Freakes' daughter who married a Buckinghamshire vicar, Susan Wolton - a wife, daughter and daughter-in-law of bishops - and Dorothy Jegon, who was a wife, daughter and aunt of bishops, her husband John being a year older than her father, Richard Vaughan!

In 1599, the year when the aptly-named Mrs Worship's husband became the incumbent of the Lincolnshire parish of Croft, the far less suitably named 'Pastor John Prick's wife' was buried at Kettlebaston Church in Suffolk. Mrs Prick was eighty and the small brass plaque memorial to her states that 'Four months and one and thirty years with him she ran her race'. Likewise, Mrs Hussey of Honington in Lincolnshire must surely have succeeded in *not* acquiring a reputation to match her surname. She shares her husband's gravestone memorial in the chancel of the village church.

Joan Churchman's maiden name was another fitting one for a clergyman's wife. She married the Anglican theologian, Richard Hooker. According to his 17th-century biographers, however, this daughter of a London Merchant Taylor was the wrong choice of wife for him. She apparently combined the qualities of being ill-tempered, 'clownish' and 'silly' with lack of good looks or riches. Her dowry was in fact the very respectable sum for those days of £700, and Hooker himself referred to Joan as 'my well-beloved wife'. Their wedding was in February 1588, seven years after the date given in a biography by Isaak Walton. Their eldest son was born and died around the time of their first wedding anniversary - five years later than an incident alleged by Walton that Joan bossed her husband to rock the cradle of one of their offspring at his parish of Drayton Beauchamp, Buckinghamshire. Two of Hooker's friends and pupils, who were visiting him then, are supposed to have departed in disgust when he complied with her request.

Such defamation of Joan seems to have stemmed partly from dislike of her and the Churchman family by some of her husband's friends, especially George Cranmer, a great-nephew of Archbishop Thomas Cranmer. George's sister, Mrs Spenser, married the London vicar who edited the books by Richard Hooker which were published posthumously. She is thought to have passed derogatory details of Joan later to the Spensers' nephew - none other than Isaak Walton!

The Hookers' youngest daughter was only seven years old when her father died in 1600. Nonetheless Walton said that she was the wife of Ezekiel Chark, a Kentish rector allowed access by Joan to Hooker's library, of which he destroyed many unpublished manuscripts before her death five months after she was widowed. Joan actually survived her husband by three years. He had appointed her as the sole executrix of his will, a tribute to her because she and her parents had looked after him in the Churchman family home when he began writing his great defence of the Anglican Church against the Puritans, *The Laws of Ecclesiastical Politie.*

The first five volumes of this were published during his marriage to Joan and within the final decade of Elizabeth I's long nourishing of the Church. Hooker's work enhanced the Virgin Queen's sense of England, in that it set the course for her national Church's theology. Modern historical studies indicate that his marriage to Joan was happy, and thanks to these, she has at last been acknowledged for the important part which she played. Joan provided the background support and nurturing which enabled her husband to help Elizabeth strengthen the Church of England.

CHAPTER 5

A Pair of Stocking Tales

An Elizabethan story often quoted by historians is that of the Queen and her first pair of silk stockings. These were hand-knitted and presented to her in 1560 by her silk-woman, Mrs Montague, while Elizabeth was with the men she called her "Eyes", Lord Robert Dudley, and her "Spirit", Sir William Cecil. At first she could not be persuaded to try the stockings on, as she believed they were too flimsy to wear.

Her favourite, Robert, replied in the requisite way so appealing to Elizabeth, by insisting that she was beautiful and a fairy queen needing only "this gossamer wear to perfect fairy attire". Less pleasing to the royal ears was the opinion of Sir William Cecil, who agreed with her that no person's leg could fit into them. Even if hers could, she risked angering the cloth hose trade, whose stockings were worthy of being worn by everyone.

Elizabeth retired in a huff to her private apartments with her new silk stockings and was gone for about an hour. On her return, she was in a better mood because they fitted her well. "I like them much," she declared, "because they are pleasant, fine and delicate, and henceforth I will wear no more cloth stockings."

She did bear Cecil's advice in mind, though, for she was fully aware how important the hand-knitting of cloth hose had become in several parts of her realm. This thriving industry provided extra vital income for families by employing women and girls, especially in the Midlands, East Anglia, the Yorkshire Dales, Lincolnshire and the West Country. In 1589 Elizabeth refused to grant a patent for a new invention, the framework knitting machine, because she feared it might put many hand-knitters out of work. She ordered its inventor, William Lee, to devise a machine which made silk stockings. Nine years passed before she witnessed a demonstration of Lee's machine producing a pair of silk stockings. But although these were presented to her, she still would not allow him a patent, for the same reason as last time.

Elizabeth may have heard the traditional tale of the young female hand-knitter who is said to have inspired Lee to invent his knitting machine. One version of the story gives her name as Janet Thrushton. She taught hand-knitting in the village of Calverton, Nottinghamshire, where Lee was the curate of the parish. Around 1586 he attempted to court Janet, but found himself doing so to the constant click of her knitting needles each time he visited her. It is not clear whether she continued knitting simply because she was too busy, or was trying to spurn him as a result of feeling unattracted to him or the prospect of being a clergyman's wife.

Whatever her reason, her behaviour is said to have exasperated Lee so much that he invented the framework knitting machine in a fit of pique to deter such female hard-heartedness in future! The sight of his mother and sisters spinning and knitting was also likely to have been a familiar scene to him during his childhood, and provided the basis of his knowledge of the industry – or even a further incentive for a machine to speed up the production process.

The Queen's lack of encouragement did not prevent his invention from revolutionizing the hosiery industry in the following century or influencing its modern high speed machinery. The coat-of-arms of the Company of Framework Knitters in London recalls the story by depicting a Tudor clergyman and a young woman, who holds a spindle and a pair of knitting needles.

Arms of the Company of Framework Knitters

CHAPTER 6

'Excellent Skill' in Needlework

'This worke beseemeth Queenes of great renowne
And Noble Ladies of a high degree:
Yet not exempt for maids of any Towne,
For all may learn that thereto willing be ...'

Isabel, Countess of Rutland, had cause to enjoy reading this rhyme in the introduction to a pattern book called *Needleworkes*, which was published in 1596. The book was dedicated to her! Its author, William Barley, worded his tribute directly: 'I could not be persuaded of a more sufficient Patronesse than your Honour, whose excellent skill in curious Needleworks is made knowne by many other personages.'

Needlecrafts such as embroidery, sewing and lace-making gained added popularity in Tudor times from royal ladies, including Catherine of Aragon, Mary, Elizabeth and Mary Queen of Scots, who were all very gifted needlewomen. Tudor embroidery was often stitched in bright and beautiful colours. Some designs were described by Shakespeare as 'Nature's own shape, of bud, birch, branch or berry' and art 'that e'en sisters the natural roses'. Countess Isabel's own talent was part of a strong, practical ability for which she was noted even in her youth as a maid of honour to Queen Elizabeth. For instance, when she and Edward Manners, 3rd Earl of Rutland, fell in love, Isabel wrote to her parents not only to tell them of her happiness but also to ask how much her dowry would be!

Her mother, Lady Julyan Holcroft, replied with some amusement from the family home at Vale Royal in Cheshire, to the Earl himself: 'She desires a very great sum of money, but says that you will marry her, whether I give anything or no.' He had been regarded as one of the most eligible bachelors at Court, and when Isabel and her companion maids of honour had chatted while they spent time together at their embroidery frames, they had often speculated about who would be his wife. Many years later, Isabel may well have appreciated the first pattern in *Needleworkes*, for it depicted Cupid in the centre of a lace pattern and possibly alluded to her marriage being a love-match.

As the Countess of Rutland, she lived at Belvoir Castle in Leicestershire. Her proficiency in needlework no doubt found frequent use, with such a large household to supervise. 16th-century documents such as the letters of the Johnson family, merchant drapers who lived at Glapthorn, Northamptonshire, in the 1550s, give glimpses of the sheer amount of needlework required in the manor house there. A young wife called Sabine Johnson and her maids sewed and embroidered clothes for the family and servants, and sometimes as presents. In addition, her letters mentioned them working on household items like cushions and bedding. Once, when some much-needed sewing thread for New Year's gifts did not arrive until Sabine's husband John brought it home with him for Christmas, she berated him in no uncertain terms for allowing her no time to make any presents for family and friends!

Besides the tangible creative and practical results of various forms of needlework, part of its attraction for many women was in its social side, in the female camararderie which it could bring as they worked together at a potentially relaxing activity. Being very much deemed to be women's work in the male-dominated Tudor world, here was an art-form in which women could be left to their own devices in more ways than one.

At times of adversity, though, the therapeutic effects of needlework offered their own special significance as a form of consolation. The well-known examples of Mary Queen of Scots' needlework on display at Oxburgh Hall in

A needlewoman at work during an historical reconstruction

Norfolk, for instance, indicate how productive she was in the early part of her captivity in England, when one observer noted that 'all day she wrought with her needle'. When tragedy touched Isabel's life, she too turned naturally to the crafts at which she was so highly accomplished. The kneeling figure of a young girl on her tomb in Bottesford Church, Leicestershire, commemorates her only daughter, Elizabeth Manners, who married and had a son, but shortly afterwards died at the age of fifteen. This happened only two years after Isabel was widowed in the spring of 1587.

Her epitaph extols her as an 'honourable wief'. She gained total possession of all her own 'garments and apparel' and jewels as a result of her beloved husband's will. With the Earl of Rutland's many other bequests to her as well, Isabel evidently made certain of a secure future for herself. She had his coach with horses, '500 good ewes', corn, grain, brass and pewter utensils, furniture and even sheets and bed-hangings, which she may have sewn and embroidered through her own efforts.

Lace pattern with 'Cupid' motif, in Needleworkes

In the same year as *Needleworkes* was published, Isabel's memories of her life at Court before her noble marriage were recalled when her beautiful niece, Mary Fitton, was appointed to be a royal maid of honour. Mary was the younger daughter of Isabel's sister Alice and lived at the Fittons' attractive black-and-white ancestral home at Gawsworth Hall in Cheshire. If this country girl, who was inexperienced in the devious ways of Queen and Court, needed sympathetic advice and guidance over such matters, who else could help her but her admired Aunt Isabel?

Alas for such hopes! Mary did not remain inexperienced for long. She was lively, outgoing and a very good dancer, and she soon acquired an elderly, very love-sick devotee called Sir William Knollys. Her disdainful treatment of him appears to have influenced Shakespeare, for the besotted Sir William provided the role-model for the character, Malvolio, in *Twelfth Night*. Mary herself was long reputed to be the Dark Lady of Shakespeare's *Sonnets*, despite her fair-skinned complexion, auburn hair and grey-blue eyes. The Bard wrote that the mysterious Dark Lady had raven black brows, and although she had a talent for playing music, he could see 'a thousand errors' in her appearance:

> *'If snow be white, why then her breasts are dun;*
> *If hairs be wires, black wires grow on her head.*
> *I have seen roses damask'd, red and white,*
> *But no roses see I in her cheeks;*
> *And in some perfumes is there more delight*
> *Than in the breath that from my mistress reeks ...'*

The historian A.L. Rowse put forward the name of Emilia Bassano or Lanier, as matching this description far more closely. She was descended from a family of Italian musicians.

Mary Fitton's mother, Lady Alice, must surely have much preferred her sister Isabel's literary connection with

Needleworkes, to that of her wayward daughter with Shakespeare. In 1601, Mary was ordered to leave the Court in disgrace for becoming pregnant by the future Earl of Pembroke, who would not marry her. Her baby was still-born and she went on to have two more illegitimate children, before she eventually married their father Sir Richard Leveson's friend, William Polewheele.

Here was more than a hint of the 'lewd world' referred to on the epitaph of Dame Dorothy Selby of Ightham Mote in Kent! This praises Dorothy's needlework for turning such a world 'into a Golden Age', though unfortunately she died from an infection caused by pricking her finger with a needle while she was sewing.

Countess Isabel died in January 1606 and was mourned by the long-suffering Alice, who finally dissociated herself from her daughter Mary that year. Alice could continue to bask in the family pride that William Barley's *Needleworkes* addressed Isabel in truth as a 'most vertuous Lady', but this feeling was marred because the same could never be said of their other former royal maid of honour, Mary Fitton.

Tomb of Isabel, Countess of Rutland, at Bottesford Church, Leicestershire

CHAPTER 7

Gangster Moll

A double difficulty faced Mary Frith's parents when they placed her as a domestic servant in a London household - she detested housework and childminding! Her mother and father were merely following the conventional, and indeed the only, way for daughters of Tudor tradesmen. But Mary Frith was not conventional. Even if she had been their son, it is possible that she would not have wished to work in her family's shoemaking business. She was, however, very genuinely attached to her native city of London and to keeping pets.

Mary was born in 1584. A near-contemporary biography leaves no doubt that she was a tomboy in childhood - 'a very tomrig or rumpscuttle' is its lively description of her. The usual girlish activities such as stitching at an embroidery sampler or helping round the house were definitely not for her! She much preferred the rough and tumble of sports and play considered then as only suitable for boys. She wore the male attire of doublet, breeches and hose from early in life, and seeing herself as one of the boys, she learnt to swagger and swear with ease. When she grew up, she had no fear of using a sword, probably an indication that fencing lessons were part of her formal education.

Females were not necessary excluded from swearing profusely - Queen Elizabeth, for instance, was noted for it. If Mary Frith had been able to enjoy the company of well-educated and intelligent women like the Queen, perhaps she would not have shunned other females so much. Her social rank restricted such a possibility in her day, though, and her hatred of the mostly domestic chatter of women from the same background as herself quickly proved to be another problem in the life of chores chosen for her by her parents. Whether she was dismissed from her job or left of her own accord, the long skirts and apron of a maidservant's outfit were eagerly discarded and Mary returned home, clad again in men's clothes.

Whatever family row ensued, her homecoming seems to have been a temporary arrangement too. With her parents in despair of her and the future uncertain because opportunities for women were so limited, a further show of bravado was called for. She soon gained a nickname which told its own tale - "Moll Cutpurse" - a pickpocket at the start of her life in London's criminal underworld. Her notorious new name came on the strength of her ability. She never followed the female roles such as that of a prostitute, or mistress of a male gangster, which were later associated with the word 'moll'. Having always accepted herself as the equal of her male contemporaries, she baulked at being under the control of any of them! Her reputation, in contrast, included being called a bully. Whether this was true or conjectured, it gave some grudging recognition to her personal inclination to be in charge of her own gang.

Her transition from being Moll Cutpurse the pickpocket to Moll the gang leader was swift. When she was in her early twenties, a comedy play called *The Roaring Girle* by Thomas Middleton and Thomas Dekker was based on her. Highway robbery, forging, receiving and handling stolen goods, pawnbroking and innkeeping were amongst her various activities. On Sundays, she distributed food and alms acquired from some of her loot to the inmates of London prisons. She may also have been the first woman to be paid for a public performance on stage - one document referred to her appearance at the Fortune Theatre in her usual attire, playing a lute while she regaled the audience with lewd songs and speeches. Such singing and swearing filled many an evening of drinking and tobacco-smoking with her circle of male friends. Moll was 'mightily taken' with smoking a pipe, all the more so because she was probably right in claiming to be the first female smoker. She believed that puffing regularly on her clay pipe of tobacco was beneficial to her health.

The general populace of London regarded this home-grown woman gangster in their midst with a mixture of curiosity and awe. She and her gang had their headquarters at her house in Fleet Street, only a short distance from the scenes of her childhood exploits around her parents' home and business in the Barbican. Although Moll was very much the local girl made bad rather than good, she became a popular figure while she was still young and this helped her when she faced a court and trial at the age of twenty-seven.

There was no denying that Moll was guilty of the offence for which she stood accused in a Church of England court. She was convicted of dressing like a man! Her punishment certainly put a stop to this, at least for a short while. She was sentenced to do public penance wearing a white sheet, the requisite garb for this form of ordeal. The venue was Paul's Cross and Moll fortified herself heavily with drink beforehand. But she need not have worried about the attitude of the crowd of onlookers, mostly fellow-Londoners who were far more interested in anything she said than they were in the long-winded sermon preached against her by an Oxford minister called Radcliffe.

Mary Frith was yet more of an exception in Elizabethan England because of her soft spot for animals. As well as dogs and horses, her menagerie of pets included an eagle, a monkey and even a lion. She reached the great age for bygone times of seventy-five, never regretting that she had rejected the usual path of life for a shoemaker's daughter. Her burial brought her earthly existence full circle, though, for it took place in the very same church where she had been baptized, St Bride's in Fleet Street.

St Paul's Cross

CHAPTER 8

'Helpful with Phisick'

A form of massage called 'frictions' was to be used from the neck to the foot in the treatment of falling sickness, according to one of the many Tudor women healers, Lady Grace Mildmay of Apethorpe in Northamptonshire. Her approach would nowadays be termed holistic, in that she was aware of how a patient's diet and emotional state can help or hinder the chances of recovery from illness. For falling sickness, she advised abstinence from eating fried meats and also from dwelling on melancholy thoughts. She attempted to treat sufferers of a variety of physical and mental disorders, but admitted that this particular ailment was 'difficult to cure'.

Learning about the practice of 'phisick', using mainly herbal remedies, was an essential part of girls' education. Qualified physicians were few in country areas, so the basic medical services provided by untrained local women was vital. Their work has mostly had little acknowledgement and was rarely documented. Grace Mildmay was exceptional, both for the high regard of male doctors for her healing expertise and the fact that she wrote down her remedies, including some collected from other women. She mentioned several ingredients in her salves and potions which have remained familiar and popular herbs, such as camomile, rosemary and St John's wort. She also used the unfamiliar, but decidedly less mundane name of pellitory-of-the-wall for nettles.

Grace paid tribute in her memoirs to her cousin and childhood governess, Mistress Hamblyn, whose influence on her was profound. This lady had 'a good knowledge of phisick and surgerie' and her writing ability was equal to that of many well-educated men. Grace's mother, Anne Sharington, had brought up Mistress Hamblyn and entrusted her wholeheartedly with the education of Grace and two other daughters, Ursula and Olive. Born in about 1552, Grace was the second of the Sharington sisters. Her father Sir Henry inherited Lacock Abbey in Wiltshire when she was a year old and it became their main family home. Here, Mistress Hamblyn regularly set Grace the task of reading Tudor medical books, especially *Turner's Herball,* which she continued to consult throughout her adult life.

Lacock Abbey, Wiltshire

That life began for Grace at the early age of fifteen, when her parents arranged her marriage to Anthony Mildmay of Apethorpe. She had an inauspicious start to living in her new home with her parents-in-law. Her husband was often absent on travels abroad, which caused the young couple to be in debt. He had been reluctant to marry and only went through with the wedding because of family pressure. Despite his neglect of her, Grace tried to heed her mother-in-law's advice to be a dutiful and obedient wife.

Other young girls would have baulked at what she herself referred to as her 'solitarinesse' in the first few years at Apethorpe, but the grounding she had received at Lacock from her mother and much-loved governess stood her in good stead for filling her days with 'many good delights'. She enjoyed drawing, playing her lute, singing, designing her own items of needlework and reading, especially her 'books of phisick'. She also began to gain practical experience of what she is praised for on her epitaph - being 'charitably helpful with phisick ... to any in misery'. The best doctors that Grace knew influenced her too in achieving an important role for herself through her medical services to the local populace.

Grace's memoirs reveal the major impact on her of following her mother's example of meditating each day on extracts from the Bible. This put good thoughts in her mind and so built up a positive outlook, which not only benefited her own sense of well-being but added to her understanding of alleviating illness. Grace knew from her own taste of adversity how optimism can help a person to rise above this. She recognized too that negative emotions may have a harmful effect on health, even being a contributory cause of ailments. Problems such as facial spots and pimples were described by her as the result of sinful thoughts, for instance, and she believed that 'godly living' was a much better cure for spots than the external application of skin remedies.

Fourteen years of marriage went by before Grace gave birth to her only child, a daughter named Mary. In the meantime, her older sister Ursula died childless and the youngest of the Sharington sisters, Olive, made a marriage which contrasted greatly with that of Grace. Olive suffered a bout of loneliness during her teens, but not because of being neglected by a husband. The cause instead was that her father forbade her to meet her sweetheart, John Talbot, and certainly not to marry him.

One evening in 1574, however, Olive was in the house at Lacock when she chanced to see John walking outside. She decided at once to defy her father and go into the grounds to talk to John, so she called to him that she would leap down. She did this from the battlements at the top of the house. The wind spread her long skirts out like a parachute and John rushed to try and catch her in his arms. But she landed so fully on him that she knocked him out! Mistress Hamblyn's medical skills were needed then to revive him. Olive's father probably also had to be treated - for shock at what she had done. He relented and gave his blessing to her love-match.

Grace later left all her medical papers to her daughter, as well as her share of the Sharington lands. Her husband inherited Apethorpe in 1589 and at last, after living there for over twenty years, she was in charge of the large household. Her papers mention that she had a housekeeper called Bess who sometimes helped with the time-consuming process of preparing medicines through various stages of infusion and distillation.

Some of the ingredients used by Grace Mildmay were new in Tudor times - amongst them were opium, hart's horn and oil of guaiacum. She included opium in a painkiller called laudanum, but ensured that another of its contents, oil of nutmegs, was not added for her female patients, because she regarded this as risky. Also perilous, in her estimation, were any attempts at trying to cause an abortion by the drastic method of soaking a salted sponge on a stick with oil of guaiacum and then inserting this into the womb (the usual way was to drink rue, or occasionally another herb called savin).

Hart's horn featured in a grim remedy for jaundice passed on by 'olde Mistresse Basshe' and recommended by Grace as 'verie goode' It involved digging a great hole, into which a large amount called a peck of snails was poured and roasted alive in charcoal till all noises from them ceased. Then they were brought out, thoroughly cleaned of their green froth and bruised with their shells in a stone mortar, before the hart's horn and other ingredients including celandine (believed to alleviate this disease because its boiled roots were the same yellow colour), cloves and rosemary flowers were put in, along with sixteen pints of strong ale. When this concoction was later distilled, a dose of two spoonfuls of it were to be given to a sufferer in the mornings, with four spoonfuls of ale or white wine, and treatment was to continue with a two-hour sleepless fast.

Only two other Tudor women have left surviving

Tomb of Lady Grace Mildmay, Apethorpe Church, Northamptonshire

memoirs - Lady Margaret Hoby and Lady Anne Clifford. The personal observations and recollections of both these Yorkshirewomen were expressed in diaries and Margaret Hoby wrote in hers that she was also a frequent reader of *Turner's Herball*, which she called her 'arball'. She provided medical assistance to inhabitants of the area around her home at Hackness, near Scarborough. Her patients included women in childbirth, a neighbour with an injured arm and a manservant who had accidentally cut his foot with a hatchet. She read to a sick maid, gave herbs from her garden to a woman from a nearby village, and unlike Grace Mildmay, she sometimes performed surgery.

Margaret's own tendency to suffer ill-health probably made her very sympathetic towards others who needed medical attention. She was a victim of toothache, headaches, stomach pains and colds. In her diary, she recorded her belief that these infirmities were God's punishment for her sins. The entry for Friday 17th August 1599 referred to her weak stomach and a headache after dinner, from which she recovered when she realized how she had transgressed. She was apparently less inclined to keep up her diary when she felt better, as she did in 1602, a year of gaps between the dates of diary-writing. Only the year before, on 13th July, an attack of colic had left her so debilitated that she had been unable to do her daily spiritual devotions of private morning and evening prayers, and reading from the Bible. Perhaps improved health helped Margaret to concentrate more easily on such matters and then to boost herself further with a more congenial frame of mind, like that gained by Grace Mildmay from her religious meditations.

Margaret's mother, Thomasine Dakins, lived about twelve miles from Hackness, in the family's manor houses at Linton and Newton. The diary mentions their regular visits to each other, but does not say whether Margaret learned her medical knowledge from her mother. Several years of her upbringing were spent in the Puritan Countess of Huntingdon's household at Ashby-de-la-Zouch Castle, Leicestershire, and the routines of Margaret's own household at Hackness reflected her education by the Countess, who prided herself on knowing how to 'govern young gentlewomen'. Like the Countess, Margaret was childless and she in her turn received some local girls into her service, where they learnt household management in preparation for their future as married women. She penned in her diary that in February 1603, one of these girls, Mercy Hunter, became the second wife of the Hackness chaplain, Richard Rhodes, and her sister Elizabeth then replaced her amongst Margaret's attendants. Whatever 'knowledge of phisick' this next generation acquired during their time with her, however, is not recorded.

Documents from different parts of Tudor England sometimes contained the names of women healers and their work, albeit briefly. Mother Coll of Norwich and Widow Yard of Barnstaple in Devon, for instance, were each credited with healing leg injuries of female patients.

Mother Edwin of London cured a teenage boy's hernia and Widow Mercer of Chester was well-practised in treating madness. Isabel Warwick of York and Margaret Gifford of Cosford, Staffordshire, both had a reputation for being good surgeons (*this* Margaret's skirts were patched at the knees due to the long time she knelt to say her daily prayers!). It is a pity that more of the unsung and possibly outstanding medical women were not given lasting praise for their efforts, like Grace Mildmay, Margaret Colfe of Lewisham (see the chapter on *Mrs Minister*) and Joyce Tomer of Coventry. Joyce's patron, Sir Edward Saunders, placed a brass memorial to her in the chancel of Weston-under-Wetherley Church, Warwickshire, after she died just before Christmas in 1566:

> *'Here lieth Joyce Tomer, slayne by death, that had of physsicke*
> *   skylle*
> *Whose losse these comfortes Saunders shewes as tokens of*
> *   good will.'*

CHAPTER 9

Women in the World of Books

Female authors whose work was published in Tudor times were very few. Margaret Tyler realized only too well that she risked facing prejudice when her English translation of a Spanish romance, *A Mirrour of Princely Deedes and Knighthood,* appeared in 1578. She justified herself in the Preface for undertaking an occupation which was seen so much as exclusively for men. At the same time, she politely challenged why this situation should continue to prevail against women.

A foretaste of future feminist writing came just over a decade later with the publication of a pamphlet, *Jane Anger, her Protection for Women.* This spoke strongly in women's favour and denounced the wrong of sexual infidelities committed by some men. But even so, its author felt the need to write under her pseudonym and otherwise remain anonymous.

In 1590, one of Jane Anger's publishers, Thomas Orwin, became the third husband of Joan Robinson, who had long been associated with the world of printing and publishing. All her husbands were printers and ran their business on the same premises during their marriage to her. The Registers of the London Stationers' Company document the active involvement of women in this industry and reveal, for instance, that on 1st December 1595, Joan Orwin and her son were fined twenty shillings 'for printing books disorderly'. Half of this amount was paid in the following month and half was remitted.

Joan at last took control of the family business herself after Thomas Orwin died in 1593. She kept it going until her son was old enough to take over. She was in charge of an apprentice called Rafe Hoolme, who came from Cheshire, and the books printed and published by her husbands - including such erudite titles as *Master Calvin's*

Catechism and *Virgil in Latin* - became her property. Modern studies of late Elizabethan London have found that, like Joan, other widows tended to acquire their next spouse from the same or a related trade or craft instead of continuing with their deceased husband's business for long in their own right. Such a situation brought an important element of continuity to several established printing and publishing businesses. Frances Simson ran her late husband Gabriel's business from 1600-2 until it passed to her two subsequent husbands, and Alice Burton, who also married three printers, experienced the last two becoming Masters of the Stationers' Company in 1595 and 1603. Joan Butter printed and published for four years from 1590-4 before she remarried, but her second printer husband died eight years later and the Registers listed her as Joan Newbery when she then resumed charge of the business.

It is a curious fact that almost a third of the women printers and publishers whose first names are recorded, were called Joan. Alice and Elizabeth were popular names amongst the rest of them. Sometimes the Registers refer to women members simply as 'widow', followed by their surname. Widow Dawson, whose husband had succeeded his uncle, continued his business with her nineteen year old son who was 'bredd to ye trade'. The widows of Thomas Vautrollier and Robert Robinson were not mentioned as trading independently, but when each of them remarried in the 1590s, their new husbands followed the well-worn pattern of succeeding to the predecessor's already existing business.

Some women ensured continuity in the opposite way, however, by remaining as widows and being head of the deceased husband's business for a decade or more. Amongst them were Joan Broome, Agnes Pickering, Alice Gossop, Alice Wolfe, Elizabeth Oliffe and Margaret Allde, who 'keepes her trade by her sonne', according to the Registers. Alice Wolfe played her part in continuity which lasted for most of Queen Elizabeth's reign and several years beyond. Her husband John had been apprenticed to one of the founders of the Stationers' Company, John Day, in 1562 and she continued his business for twelve years after he died in 1601. As 'Mistress Woolf' she was mentioned during that year when her apprentice, William Whitby, became a Freeman of the Company and a qualified printer and publisher, an occasion for a celebratory meal.

The Stationers' Company was incorporated in Mary Tudor's reign in 1556. At the outset, Elizabeth Toy ran her late husband's business from 1556-8, before it passed to her son. The Registers tell that she paid eleven shillings for a new glass window in the Stationers' Hall in 1556 and contributed towards the cost of the annual Company dinner even in 1559, when her responsibility for the family business had ceased. Elizabeth's son paid £4 to the Company ten years later as 'bequest of Elyzabeth Toye Wydowe late of London stacioner Deceased' - a rare written record of a Tudor woman's occupation.

There are several instances of widows assigning to other Company members the future production of books 'lawfully apperteyning' formerly to their husbands. Apprentices were sometimes transferred or 'put over' to other printers too, so that they could serve the rest of their apprenticeship elsewhere if a widow stopped trading. Occasionally, though, an apprentice was transferred from a man to a woman, as happened when Robert Weekes was 'put over' from William Lloyd to Joan Bourne for three years from 1593. One entry in the Registers shows a clear return to the position of subservience when a widow remarried: in July 1578, 'Mistres harrison' sold various publications herself of her late husband Luke's to a printer called Thomas Woodcock. But from November of that year, the consent of her second husband, Robert Farmer, was required for the transfer of two of Luke Harrison's apprentices to other printers.

Widowhood was not always a guarantee of complete independence in decision-making, however, as Helen Ward found. Although one of her husband's relatives,

George Ward, was officially apprenticed to her, he had to 'serve all his tyme' with a type-founder called Benjamin Sympson and learn only the 'founder's art'.

John Day's widow, Alys, was referred to as 'Mistress Day alias Stone' when she was 'putting over' her apprentice, John Danter, in April 1588. She seems therefore to have remarried within four years of losing her first husband, as hinted on her epitaph to him in the delightful church at Little Bradley, Suffolk:

> *'Als was the last encreaser of his stoore*
> *Who mourning long for being left alone*
> *Sett up this toombe, herself turned to a stone.'*

This memorial also details that both she and Day's first wife were 'pertekers of his payne' in assisting him with his business concerns. Day printed and published many of the leading books of Elizabethan times, including *Foxe's Book of Martyrs*, which he appears to have instigated John Foxe to write about the Protestants martyred under Queen Mary, 'to show what bloudi actes were donne'. As for the Days' former apprentice, John Danter, who died in 1599, the Registers not surprisingly list 'Widow Danter' as taking over the business after him.

CHAPTER 10

Marian Martyrs

In the summer of 1553, many of the new Queen Mary's subjects were too young to remember a time when the country had followed what was known then as the 'old faith', the Roman Catholic religion which she still practised devoutly. Joan Waste of Derby was one who could not accept a religion contrary to the Protestant faith in which she had always worshipped, and she heard of others too who were so steadfast in the same beliefs as hers that they were fleeing into exile or else suffering imprisonment or death.

The 16th century tower of All Saints' Church (nowadays Derby Cathedral) was built a few years before Joan was born, but she never saw this during her short life, not even when she was led into the crowded church on the day of her execution - for she was born blind. Joan's ordeal was singled out in *Foxe's Book of Martyrs* as one of especially 'unmerciful cruelty'. She was amongst about sixty Protestant women who were burnt at the stake between 1555 and 1558. The burning of so many in so little time caused revulsion and outrage in a society which was far from squeamish. Like the majority of victims, Joan Waste was poor. She was threatened with 'grievous imprisonments, torments and death' by the Bishop of Lichfield and Coventry, and his chancellor, unless she renounced her religion. But she told them that 'by God's assistance, she was ready to yield up her life in that faith'. Martyrdom seemed better to her than existing with 'an evil conscience'.

Joan was only twenty-two years old when she was condemned to death in 1556. On 1st August she was made to stand in front of the pulpit in All Saints', before a large congregation, and was subjected to a sermon which harangued her for denying the Catholic doctrines. Her physical disability was likened to being 'blind in the eyes of her soul' and she was further denounced that as her body would soon be consumed with material fire, so her soul should be burnt in hell with everlasting fire. Those present also heard that it was unlawful for anyone to pray for her.

As Joan prepared for death at an execution site called the Windmill Pit, however, she asked the onlookers to pray *with* her. She held her brother's hand and said 'such prayers as she had learned and cried upon Christ to have mercy on her'. The entry in the parish registers recording her death acknowledged her as a martyr. Of the female executions, hers was the furthest north. Most of the women martyrs came from staunchly Protestant areas of East Anglia, London and Kent, where they sometimes outnumbered the men at the burning of several people.

The horrific executions to the furthest south involved a Guernsey mother, her two daughters - and a new-born baby. Katherine Cawches perished at St Peter's Port in July 1556 with her daughters, Willemine Gilbert and Perotine Massey, on either side of her. In the midst of the flames, Perotine gave birth to a son. The baby was moved to safety, but being regarded as a 'heretic's brat', he was soon

Burning of the three women of Guernsey

84

thrown back into the fire by order of the island's bailiff.

In Sussex, as well as in Kent, London and Essex, there were other instances of members of the same families suffering martyrdom together. Margery Moris and her son were amongst ten victims in one fire at Lewes in June 1557, the other women being Thomasine a Wood and two named only as 'Ashdon's wife' and 'Grove's wife'. Twenty year old Rose Allin of Essex, her mother Alice Munt and her stepfather were arrested in Colchester in February of that year. They were marched to London under armed guard with nineteen other Protestants, all pinioned together, and examined on their faith by the infamous Bishop, "Bloody" Bonner. They were released on condition that they attended the Catholic services in future, but were shortly forced into hiding because they remained absent from church. Foxe related that when they were found, Alice was very ill and sent Rose to fetch her some water to drink.

As the young woman returned, carrying this in a stone vessel with one hand and a lighted candle in the other, one of the Catholics surrounding the house demanded that she tell her parents to be "better Catholic people". Rose replied that she hoped God would "not suffer them to err" and added that "with what you call heresy, I worship my Lord God". She heard the man retort that she would burn and he took the candle from her. Egged on by his colleagues, he held her wrist and burnt the candle cross-wise over the back of her hand, 'till the very sinews cracked asunder'. He kept asking, "Why wilt thou not cry? Thou young hussy, why wilt thou not cry?" She answered several times that she had no cause, "but rather to rejoice" - clearly an example of the fortitude noted by John Foxe in many of the female martyrs with a rather condescending respect in remarks such as: 'Their constancy in suffering was greatly wondered at, though but women, they so manfully stood to the confession of God's word ...'

Rose Allin was eventually pushed away violently by her tormentor and had to endure 'very insulting language'.

She and her parents were burnt at Colchester on 2nd August 1557, the same day as seven other Protestants, including Helen Ewring, Agnes Silverside and Elizabeth Folks, who was also aged only twenty. Margaret Thurston, who had been arrested with her husband at the same time and place as Rose and her family, was burnt the following month with Agnes Bongeor, the widow of one of the men burnt on the 2nd. Margaret's husband had died in prison. Agnes had expected to die with hers and on that day, she gave up the baby she had been breastfeeding in prison 'to another nurse'. She had also put on a smock which she had prepared specially for her death, then found that her execution was deferred because her name was misspelt in the warrant. The deep sense of anti-climax which then beset her, combined with her grief at losing her husband and baby, severely tested her faith. Foxe wrote that a visiting friend helped Agnes to 'find comfort in reading and prayer' for the few remaining weeks of her life.

Of the four women commemorated on the martyrs' memorial at Staplehurst in Kent, Alice Potkins also died in prison, 'famished most unmercifully' at Canterbury Castle. (Prisoners had to buy their own food in those days or else they starved). She told her interrogators that she was aged forty-nine "according to my old life", but since she became a Protestant, "only one year old". Joan Bradbridge, who was young and single, and Katherine Allen, commemorated with her husband Edmund, were amongst the seven martyrs - five women and two men - at King's Meadow, Maidstone, on 18th June 1557. These included another married couple, Petronil and Walter Appleby, another blind girl, eighteen year old Elizabeth Lewis and 'John Manning's wife'.

The fourth woman on the Staplehurst memorial was listed only as 'Benden's wife' when she was burnt at Canterbury twelve days later with three men and three women: 'Wilson's wife' and two widows of martyrs, Barbara Final and 'Bradbridge's widow'. Mrs Benden's

Martyrs' memorial at Staplehurst, Kent

first name, Alice, became known because Foxe could not ignore her ill-treatment during her imprisonment.

Unlike many of the women martyrs, Alice went against her husband's wishes by continuing her Protestant faith. Cases such as hers raised the question of why harsh treatment was used against married women in Queen Mary's religious persecutions, as their husbands legally bore responsibility for them. Alice was first imprisoned in the autumn of 1556 for refusing to attend Mass at Staplehurst Church. Her husband Edward obtained her release after a fortnight, but she still stayed away from the Catholic forms of worship. Another two weeks passed, and on the Sunday her husband was influenced by some of the other parishioners to agree that she should be sent to jail again. He was even reputed to have accepted money to take her there. But Alice 'chose rather to commit herself' to imprisonment at Canterbury Castle 'than that the world should bear witness against her husband of so wicked a deed'. This time there was no hope of release, as her husband found when he petitioned for this in the following January. He then said that if Alice's brother could be kept from her, 'she would turn' her religious views.

Orders were given for the arrest of her brother if he came to see her. As a means of attracting visits from him, Alice was put into an underground cell called Monday's Hole which was only lit by a window from a courtyard above. Her brother was unable to help her, except for the occasion very early one morning when he placed some money in a loaf of bread and reached this down to her on a pole. After she had been in this cell for nine weeks, lying cold and hungry on a little straw between a pair of stocks and a wall, and never changing her clothes, Alice not surprisingly became 'a very piteous and loathsome creature to behold'. In this state, she was asked if she would now return to Staplehurst and go to church. She pointed out how painful each movement was for her as a result of her time in Monday's Hole and answered, "I am thoroughly persuaded by the great extremity that you have already showed me, that you are not of God and I see that you seek my utter destruction." Although her subsequent confinement until her martyrdom was less rigorous, poor Alice's skin 'did peel and scale off as if she had been poisoned by some mortal venom'.

The legal subjection of wives is clearly illustrated in the proceedings against Joyce Lewis of Warwickshire. The 'furiousness' of her husband Thomas forced her to attend Mass at the little village church in Mancetter, which now has a memorial to her. But the ordeal of her neighbour, Robert Glover, who was seized from his sick-bed and taken off to prison before his martyrdom, appears to have given Joyce the courage to follow her conscience. She expressed her displeasure by turning her back towards the holy water when it was sprinkled over the congregation. Because of her rank as a gentlewoman, the local bishop gave her a month's respite for 'so despising the sacraments' and her husband was ordered to bring her before the bishop again at the end of that time, on pain of forfeiting £100. Several of Joyce's friends urged Thomas Lewis to risk forfeiting the money rather than 'cast his own wife into the fire' by obeying the bishop's orders, but he declined to lose 'anything for her sake'.

Joyce's prison in Lichfield stank so much that her maid fainted. A supportive friend called Agnes Penifather accompanied Joyce from prison to her execution in August 1557 and was later closely confined herself for refusing to do public penance in Lichfield - her punishment for drinking with Joyce to the Protestant faith. Another ten friends, mainly women, were also sentenced to do penance. Eventually, they persuaded Agnes to undergo hers.

The persecutions continued in different parts of the realm, but there was a growing and widespread feeling that the tide was gradually turning towards better times, as expressed for instance in the old rhyme, 'When people with violence are burned to death, we wish for our Elizabeth'. Unfortunately, the prevailing mood of the country could not save Alice Driver of Grosborough in Suffolk, who was burnt at Ipswich less than two weeks before Mary's death in November 1558. Alice dared to agree with public opinion during her questioning, however, by calling the Queen a Jezebel because of all the burnings. Both the ears of 'this honest poor man's daughter' were immediately cut off.

One of the last female martyrs later the same month was a 'very little' elderly woman called Mrs Prest in Exeter, Devon. She too had gained confidence from anticipating the start of Elizabeth's reign and shortly before her imprisonment, she scorned a Dutch craftsman who had repaired the noses of damaged statues in a local church. "What a madman art thou to make them new noses," she said, "which within a few days shall all lose their heads!"

Amongst the women who displayed courage during these troublous times by putting themselves at risk to visit condemned Protestants in jail, the mother of a future famous Elizabethan stepped briefly into the limelight when she went to see Mrs Prest at Exeter Prison. This lady's youngest son was then about four years old and became Sir Walter Ralegh. She had five sons by her two marriages and all her offspring were very adventurous, apparently taking after their mother rather than the two fathers. *Foxe's Book of Martyrs* quoted the words of tribute spoken by Lady Ralegh concerning Mrs Prest: "I never heard a woman of such simplicity to look on, talk so godly, so sincerely and so earnestly; insomuch, that if God were not with her, she could not speak such things, to which I am not able to answer, though I can read and she cannot."

This genuine praise from one Tudor woman about another surely speaks for itself, even though the male author of *Foxe's Books of Martyrs* persisted in saying that qualities like the boldness and fortitude of 'such weak creatures' as these Protestant women were 'manly'. Elizabeth found a far less chauvinistic way of recognizing the presence of mind shown by the hostess of the Blue Post Inn at Chester, who overheard one of her guests, Dr Henry Cole, say that he was travelling with a commission from Mary to begin persecutions in Ireland. The woman feared for her own brother's safety, so she took her chance to remove the commission secretly from a leather box and substituted for the contents of this container a pack of cards, with the knave of clubs at the top. Cole reached his destination before he discovered what she had done and his return there with a second commission was prevented by Elizabeth becoming Queen. She rewarded the Chester hostess with a pension of £40 a year.

CHAPTER 11

The Countesses and the Pearl of York

Jane Neville, Countess of Westmorland, lost her temper with her husband Charles at Brancepath Castle, County Durham, one November day in 1569. "We and our country were shamed for ever," she stormed tearfully, "that now in the end we should seek holes to creep into." She had observed that both the Earl of Westmorland and Thomas Percy, Earl of Northumberland, might back down from a threat to the power which the Neville and Percy families had enjoyed for centuries in the north of England. But her words, spoken in such frustration, provoked the two Earls into a concerted course of action, and so a woman sparked off the rebellion known as the Northern Rising against a woman - Queen Elizabeth - on behalf of another woman, the captive Mary Queen of Scots.

Both Countess Jane and the equally strong-minded Anne, Countess of Northumberland, accompanied their husbands and some three hundred armed followers to nearby Durham Cathedral on 14th November. In this beautiful and ancient place, their rebellion began in earnest. Symbols of the Catholic faith had either been defaced or destroyed there over the years, after Henry VIII became head of the Church of England. Now it was the turn of Protestant furnishings and books to be attacked. The communion table was smashed into pieces and the English Bible and Books of Common Prayer were burnt. Local people crowded in amazement by the huge rounded pillars and then took part wholeheartedly in a Catholic High Mass, which was said in Latin, with all the elaborate ceremony of days of old.

The northern rebels aimed to restore the Roman Catholic faith as well as free the Queen of Scots. Jane Neville had probably been strengthened in her resolve to achieve these by the attempts of her younger brother,

Durham Cathedral

Thomas Howard, Duke of Norfolk, to dissuade her husband from leading an open conflict. A later ballad described Queen Elizabeth's reaction when she heard about the rising:

'And like a royal queen she swore,
"I will ordain them such a breakfast
As never was in the North before".'

Jane was acknowledged to be much more fluent in Latin than her brother - a compliment paid to her by their old tutor, John Foxe. She seems to have been a star pupil whose academic ability was on a level with the educated men of the period. There was indeed a paradox that this noblewoman, who had been taught and praised by the author of such an important Protestant publication as the *Book of Martyrs*, instigated a Catholic rebellion! Those childhood years at the ancestral home, Kenninghall in Norfolk, had clearly formed her character into that of the bossy older sister, however, a trait which was accentuated by the way she easily outshone all her siblings with her superior intellect. Although the Duke was England's premier peer, he was, to Jane, still the little brother who could be a target for her criticism.

This lifelong habit surfaced in expressions of derision for what she saw as his half-heartedness towards the rebellion. After all, here was a chance to rescue the Queen of Scots, who had become Norfolk's fiancee during her brief captivity at Bolton Castle in Yorkshire, where her custodian's wife, Lady Margaret Scrope, was yet another of the Duke's influential sisters! Elizabeth had ordered Mary's removal to the Midlands, but she remained geographically closer to the predominantly Catholic northern counties than she was to the English Queen in far-off London. Countess Jane was undeterred by various royal warning signs which came from the other end of the realm.

In contrast, Elizabeth and her government had been on a kind of red alert to the prospect of trouble in the north, ever since the Scottish Queen fled into England the previous year. Elizabeth's leading subjects often found that courage failed them if they needed to tell her about their marriage plans - the Duke of Norfolk was no exception, yet she had her suspicions about his schemes, for she hinted to him that he should forget about marrying Mary. When Elizabeth discovered in the early autumn of 1569 that her advice had gone unheeded, she imprisoned him in the Tower of London and angrily summoned the Earls of Westmorland and Northumberland to Court to account for their role as the Duke's fellow-plotters in Mary's cause. They wavered anxiously over what to do, but Countess Jane was determined that her husband would not leave his centre of power to put himself in Elizabeth's and be incarcerated like the Duke.

Jane had been too full of zeal in her criticism of her brother to consider the effects on him of the pressure from Elizabeth to avoid involvement with the Queen of Scots. The impact of Jane's zeal exploding into that passionate outburst at Brancepath Castle was to be more far-reaching than she could have realized. An informant to Elizabeth's Privy Council reported that Countess Anne of Northumberland also was 'earnestly bent' towards the rebellion and had great influence over her husband. Anne rode with him and the rebel army, which increased in size as they marched south as far as Bramham Moor, the site of a medieval battle, near the Great North Road in Yorkshire. Their standard was a banner which depicted a Cross and the Five Wounds of Christ and evoked a previous time, for in 1536 the same emblems had been carried in the rebellion known as the Pilgrimage of Grace against Henry VIII. (A banner of St Cuthbert also carried then had been burnt early in Elizabeth's reign by Mrs Horne, the wife of the Puritan Dean of Durham).

Like the Pilgrimage of Grace, the Northern Rising failed and the Tudor vengeance was swift and terrible. The Nevilles and Percies never again held such sway in the north. A little over a month after the scenes in Durham Cathedral, their vast property was forfeited and the two Countesses and their husbands parted for ever. Countess Jane returned to Norfolk, but Countess Anne meanwhile fled north towards the Scottish border with the two Earls, some of their followers and a few of her own attendants. *Her* adventures were by no means over yet.

The bedraggled fugitives struggled in December weather through miles of bleak and boggy moorland to the only place of refuge for them - Liddesdale, the haunt of robbers and outlaws! They crossed over the Liddel Water into Scotland and soon encountered two of the most infamous Border thieves, Jock o'the Side and Black

Ormiston, who led them past dismal cottages of mud and stone to Jock's own hovel at a place called The Side on a nearby slope. Later, this was described as being worse than any dog kennel in England, yet it was their accommodation for the night. The dwellings of Liddesdale surely were a far cry from the luxuries of life at castles such as Alnwick and Brancepath.

Mary Queen of Scots

Countess Anne was the daughter of Edward Somerset, Earl of Worcester. She was a tall woman, like the Queen of Scots. During Mary's captivity in the north, Anne had offered to visit her in disguise as a nurse ostensibly to see a pregnant servant called Margaret Cawood, then exchange clothes with Mary and so let her escape. Anne and her husband had first visited the royal captive soon after her sensational arrival in England and they had even hoped that they would be appointed as Mary's custodians. A 17th-century Border ballad song shows the Countess as trying to persuade her husband to go to London and answer Elizabeth's summons, saying that she will accompany him. It reflects the strong element of partnership which existed in reality in the Northumberlands' marriage. However, the Earl resists his wife's advice in several verses, such as:

> 'Now nay, now nay, my lady deare;
> Far lever [rather] had I lose my life,
> Than leave among my cruel foes
> My love in jeopardy and strife.'

As Christmas 1569 approached, there was little sign of any seasonal goodwill in Liddesdale towards the weary new arrivals. Their horses were stolen and the immediate future was literally decided for them, when the two Earls were told to leave Scotland within a day or else they would be betrayed to the Scottish government by a local outlaw called Elliot. So the words in the later ballad verse were in a way partly fulfilled for Anne, as she was left reluctantly among foes 'in jeopardy and strife'. Whatever her misgivings may have been, the speedy departure of both rebel Earls from Liddesdale took priority over much time for fond farewells. The men were rushed away into a Border area known then as the Debateable Land because of uncertainties about whether it belonged to England or Scotland.

Early in January, Anne and her ladies also suddenly left Liddesdale, thanks to a successful rescue raid by some of Queen Mary's Scottish Border supporters, led by Sir Thomas Kerr of Ferniehurst, near Jedburgh. One of Elizabeth's officials wrote on 9th January 1570: 'Notwithstanding strait proclamations for not receiving or aiding the Queen's rebels within any part of Scotland ... the Countess of Northumberland was brought by Farnhurst towards Hume Castle, stayed at Roxburgh by the way, reaching Hume Friday morning, where she is yet, unless this day conveyed to Vaux Castle.'

Countess Anne's sense of relief over her rescue from such untoward surroundings by people who were loyal to the Queen of Scots was, alas, mixed with other emotions. She learnt with sorrow and anxiety that her beloved husband had become separated from the Earl of Westmorland, and he had then been betrayed 'for a sum of gold' by a man he had helped in the past. This was Hecky, or Hector Armstrong of Harlaw, near Canonbie. The Scottish Regent, the Earl of Moray, apparently intended to hand Anne's husband over to Elizabeth in exchange for Mary. Meanwhile, the Earl of Westmorland fared better and, like Anne, was in the hands of Border sympathizers who refused to give him up. An attempt to rescue the Earl of Northumberland unfortunately failed and he was imprisoned in the remote Lochleven Castle.

More turmoil spread through the Borders when the Scottish Regent was assassinated in mid-January 1570 and English troops carried out destructive raids in southern Scotland during the spring. Countess Anne faced a dilemma between accepting the Scottish government's offer of being re-united with her husband and thus risking her own freedom, or remaining free but with the possibility that their hurried goodbye embrace in Liddesdale might have been their last. She devoted herself to obtaining his release and believed that she could be more effective on his behalf if she stayed at liberty. In the summer of 1570, Anne went into exile and raised funds from Catholic supporters abroad to put together a ransom payment for his freedom. The contributors included the Pope and King Philip of Spain, but though Anne aimed high in her efforts, she was by now working against a background of rapid change.

Queen Elizabeth was excommunicated by the Pope in 1570 and her Catholic subjects were told that they no longer owed obedience to her. One of the effects of the Northern Rising was a hardening of attitudes between Catholics and Protestants. This Papal declaration ended the 'middle way' of the first eleven years of Elizabeth's reign, during which Catholics had been able to follow their own faith privately without interference, provided that they conformed outwardly to the Church of England services. The laws to punish those who refused to attend their local parish church each Sunday were strengthened and an increasing number of English 'recusants' as they were known became exiles in Catholic countries overseas.

Elizabeth put forward a rival bid to ransom the Earl of Northumberland from his Scottish captors - and her bid succeeded. The result was a stark contrast from any hoped-for exile with his wife, for he was handed over to the English Queen's officials at the Border fortress town of Berwick-on-Tweed and taken as a prisoner to York, where he was publicly beheaded. Ironically the date of his execution, 22nd August 1572, was the anniversary of the Tudor victory at the Battle of Bosworth which had brought the dynasty to the English throne. When the Earl spoke on his execution scaffold in a street called The Pavement, however, he stated defiantly that he was subject to the Pope and not to Queen Elizabeth. A sixteen year old girl who witnessed his demise was deeply moved by the event: Margaret Clitherow had lived in the narrow adjoining street, The Shambles, since her marriage to a York butcher the previous year. A few years after Northumberland's death, she became a Roman Catholic herself.

Margaret was York-born and bred. Her father, Thomas Middleton, was one of the city's wax chandlers. Although the family conformed to the Anglican Church, he was sympathetic towards the Catholic faith, like many of York's inhabitants. Margaret was eleven when he died in 1567 and her mother Jane then married an innkeeper called Henry May. The butcher's business of Margaret's own husband, John Clitherow, involved him working away from home sometimes. He was aware of how she spent part of each long working day - for instance, she took charge of his butcher's shop during his absences, as well as running their household and bringing up their children. But there were activities of which he was apparently unaware, illegal activities connected with her faith, and not surprisingly she was even advised by one of the Catholic priests she harboured not to tell her husband!

The priests' hiding-place was in the roof space of her next door neighbours' house and there was a secret door between the two dwellings. Margaret and several of her Catholic friends were imprisoned in a place called the Kidcote, near Ouse Bridge in York, for their non-attendance at Church of England services. Her stepfather took part in the arrest of two of her closest friends, Dr and Mrs Vavasour, an experience which afflicted the lady briefly with insanity and also unnerved Margaret. She was destined to be on a collision course with Henry May over religious differences. His sights were set on becoming Lord Mayor of York, so he regarded his stepdaughter's Catholicism as an impediment to his political ambitions - and that was his opinion of Margaret even before the civic authorities knew that her house was a refuge for priests.

In December 1582, Elizabeth wrote to the Mayor and Aldermen of York in strong words about their neglect of their duties in finding and bringing to justice 'all manner of Popish priests' in the city. She commanded them to be more diligent from then on and also to watch the recusant residents more closely, so that they 'may be thoroughly proceeded against according to our laws'. Only conscientiousness as expected by Her Majesty of the authorities would appease her and give her 'cause to think that you desire thereby to repair the faults of your former negligence'. Her orders were duly carried out, with the result that in addition to many imprisonments during the next decade, there were forty-one executions, including those of twenty-six priests.

Margaret continued practising her faith, undeterred by the risks she was taking - risks which increased greatly in 1585, when more severe laws made the harbouring of priests an offence which was punishable by death. She faced the ever-present danger of the 'powers-that be' in Elizabethan York turning their attention in her direction without warning at any time.

Henry May badly underestimated Margaret if he thought that she would be intimidated when he caused a search of her house to be carried out in early March of 1586. Unfortunately for her, though, a young boy was bullied with the threat of physical punishment by the officers who arrived to do the search, and in his fear he revealed the secret door and chamber to them. No priests were found there, but a chalice and vestments for use at Mass were seized. These various discoveries were deemed to be enough evidence for Margaret to be arrested on charges that 'she had harboured and maintained Jesuit and other seminary priests, traitors to the Queen's Majesty and the law'.

She appeared before judges in York's 15th-century Guildhall. When they asked her whether she was guilty or not of this indictment, she replied that she had not harboured any traitors to the Queen and therefore, "Having committed no offence, I need no trial." Several ways were attempted to make her plead: she was reminded that she had undoubtedly broken the law and must face trial, her religion was ridiculed, and the chalice and vestments from her house were produced in court. But Margaret would still not plead, and nor would she do so the next day when she was brought again before the same judges. Hints were then given of clemency if she would attend the Church of England and give the names of her friends. Her answer was ready after one of the judges pointed out that there were few witnesses against her. "I think you have no witness against me but children, whom with an apple or rod you may cause to say what you will," she observed.

In Margaret's own way of reasoning, she was saving her children by her refusal to plead - saving them from the ordeal of testifying in court. She was also protecting her next door neighbours and other Catholic friends, and priests, by keeping to herself information about those who had helped her or been helped by her in her secret work.

This approach meant sacrificing her own life, however, for the penalty incurred by declining to enter a plea was to be stripped naked and pressed to death. Margaret did not flinch when this sentence was passed on her. She told the court that she prayed for a better judgement in God's presence.

Back in her prison cell, she sewed a long linen habit to cover most of her body at her execution. All her impassioned appeals to the judges for permission to see her husband were to no avail. The few kindnesses she received during her last hours came from other women, such as her gaoler's wife, who sympathized with Margaret's request for a maid to keep her company through the night before she suffered, by providing that company herself. Even the date of Margaret's death was known as 'Lady Day', 25th March, the Feast of the Annunciation of the Blessed Virgin Mary.

The name 'Fawcett' is familiar in women's studies in modern times because of its uses as the Fawcett Society and the former name of the Women's Library, but in Margaret's story an eye-witness account tells that after she had prayed, a sheriff called Fawcett commanded the guards 'to put off her apparel'. Four other women then knelt with her to ask that 'for the honour of womanhood this might be dispensed with'. Their words fell on deaf ears, so Margaret 'requested that the women might unapparel her' while male onlookers averted their gaze.

The eye-witness did not say whether the latter part of this met with compliance, but Margaret was only undressed by the four women, who then immediately helped her to put on her linen habit. She lay calmly on the ground and joined her hands in prayer. A sharp stone 'as much as a man's fist' was placed under her back and a door was put on top of her. Fawcett ordered that her hands must be bound and two sergeants parted them and tied them to two posts. They next laid weights on her 'to the quantity of seven or eight hundredweight, which breaking her ribs, caused them to burst forth of the skin'. Margaret cried out her last words in agony, "Jesu, have mercy upon me!" About fifteen minutes after the start of these barbaric proceedings, she died.

Margaret Clitherow was the first of the three Catholic women martyrs during Elizabeth's reign and became known as the "Pearl of York". At the age of thirty, she was also younger than the others, Anne Line and Margaret Ward. All three of them were amongst the forty English martyrs canonized as saints by the Catholic Church in October 1970, just over 400 years after the Northern Rising.

By coincidence, the Countess of Westmorland was also in her early thirties at the outbreak of this doomed rebellion. There is a small effigy of her, wearing her countess's coronet, on her parents' tomb in Framlingham Church, Suffolk, close to the castle where Queen Mary Tudor gathered the army which brought to an end an earlier insurrection - the nine-days' reign of Lady Jane Grey in 1553. Both the Countesses of Westmorland and Northumberland survived into the 1590s: Jane Neville was buried in Kenninghall Church, Norfolk, but Anne Percy died in exile in France. Like Margaret Clitherow, however, she had a daughter who became a nun overseas.

CHAPTER 12

The 'Queen of the Castle'

The captive Mary Queen of Scots was filled with foreboding when a heavily armed escort set off with her from Chartley Hall in Staffordshire, where her rooms had recently been ransacked. It was 21st September 1586, and she was not told that she would be travelling for five days to face trial in the grim castle at Fotheringhay in Northamptonshire. She was only informed whether each day's journey would be long or short.

The eye-witness account in the journal of her French physician, Dominique Bourgoing, related that Mary chose

Fotheringhay Castle, Northamptonshire

to travel backwards in her coach so that she could observe what the cavalcade of guards were doing behind her. Occasionally she leant out and asked her coachman, Sharpe, what was happening ahead. At the age of forty-three, Mary was too lame with rheumatism to be able to ride and she feared being assassinated at any time - a fate which she had supposedly wished on her cousin, Queen Elizabeth, when she wrote a letter in secret code the previous July to a Derbyshire Catholic called Anthony Babington.

Mary's jailers would certainly have ordered her immediate death if she tried to escape or a rescue attempt was made on her behalf. Babington and his fellow-conspirators had aimed to risk such an attempt in what has become known to history as the Babington Plot. And for a few fleeting moments back in August, Mary even thought that a group of rescuers *had* come to free her! But the riders she had seen from a distance turned out to be quite the opposite: they had been sent by Elizabeth after the discovery of this plot. They arrested Mary's two secretaries and then took her to imprisonment at nearby Tixall Hall for two weeks, while her apartments and belongings at Chartley were searched for evidence of her involvement.

The Queen of Scots did not know that by the time of this last journey of hers alive, Babington and the other plotters had already been executed in the brutal manner of the age - or that his young widow and infant daughter, who was named Mary after the royal captive, had lost their home in Derbyshire because all his property had been forfeited to the Crown.

The first stop on Mary's journey was seven miles from Chartley at another forfeited property. She rested for a few hours at Hall Hill, Abbots Bromley, which had belonged to Lord Paget until he took part in a failed plot to rescue her in 1583 and then fled into exile. The owners of Tixall, the Bagot family, were acting as royal stewards for Hall Hill when Mary visited there. A Latin inscription on a pane of glass from this house commemorated her visit and is nowadays in the William Salt Museum at Stafford.

From Abbots Bromley the journey continued for the eleven miles to Burton-on-Trent - quite a lengthy day's travel by Elizabethan standards. Mary's deep anxiety about where she was being taken, and why, was clearly reflected in Bourgoing's account that she spent a very disturbed night's sleep at Burton. Two inns there claimed to have been the place where she stayed, the Queens' Hotel and a former hostelry called the Crown Inn. Also at Burton, dwelling in a further confiscated house of Lord Paget's, were a local brewer and his wife. This character had been referred to as 'the honest man' by Mary's jailers. She had paid him to act as the go-between for her secret correspondence with Anthony Babington. All the while, however, he had been receiving money too from Elizabeth's spymaster, Sir Francis Walsingham, who read all Mary's letters in decoded form before these were passed on to their intended recipients.

The town of Burton was additionally associated with Mary's strict Puritan custodian, Sir Amyas Paulet, for it was the birthplace of his stepmother, a devout Catholic recusant, of whom the State Papers for 1578 mentioned that she 'had mass commonly at her house' in Clerkenwell, London. One of the Scottish Queen's agents had written to the royal captive that she may perhaps 'draw some service of Poulet and some of his' through this lady's influence. Any possible influence, however, seems to have worked to Mary's detriment, in that the Catholicism of Paulet's own stepmother may have contributed to his harsh treatment of Mary herself. Although men were apparently playing the active roles in Mary's tragic story, their various connections with women sometimes determined their conduct and how or why decisions were made concerning the next four days and nights of Mary's journey to Fotheringhay. Lady Paulet's links with Burton remained strong, and she made several benefactions to the town, including the establishment of almshouses for five unmarried old women.

On Thursday 22nd September, the distance to the next stopping place, at Ashby-de-la-Zouch Castle, was about seven miles. The Puritan Earl of Huntingdon and his Countess were probably not at their Leicestershire home then, unlike the time of Mary's first overnight stay there in

1569, when Huntingdon had briefly been her custodian during the Northern Rising. In those days, she had still been an attractive young woman, hopeful of regaining her Scottish throne and succeeding to the English throne if Elizabeth died. The contrast for the ailing, middle-aged captive who made her second visit to Ashby after almost seventeen years could hardly have been greater.

Mary travelled in her cumbersome coach the following day along the route she had ridden in 1569 to Leicester, entering the town through the medieval North Gate close to the remains of Leicester Abbey. Over fifty years earlier, the great Cardinal Wolsey had died here, a prisoner also on his way to face trial for treason. Mary passed Lord's Place, the Earl of Huntingdon's town house, where she had stayed in 1569. She was next taken past the East Gate, for which the town corporation had invested in a stronger security chain during her previous visit. On the Huntingdon Tower Building, which stands on the site of Lord's Place in Leicester's High Street, a wall plaque claims that she also 'lodged here in 1586'. However, Bourgoing wrote that 'Her Majesty lodged in the hostelry of the outskirts at The Angel' - an accurate description, for the Angel Inn was situated inside the town wall close to the East Gate. Nowadays its name is recalled in 'The Angel Gateway', which is in the very centre of the modern city, like the small street of 'Eastgates' nearby.

There seems to have been a mood of sympathy for Mary amongst the townsfolk of Elizabethan Leicester, a feeling that there would be trouble around the realm if she were executed. Perhaps memories stirred for them of the sad fate of their own local royal ladies, Jane and Catherine Grey.

The fear of demonstrations in Mary's favour led to an entry in the town records that three men were paid two shillings 'for 2 nights watchinge of Sir Amias Polletts carriages'. This has led several historians to state that Mary herself stayed in Leicester for two nights, then travelled directly from there to Fotheringhay on 25th

September. Bourgoing's journal was published as long ago as the 1870s, yet the details given by this physician who had the advantage of actually being with Mary on her journey, have often been ignored. He mentioned that 24th September was a rainy day, and Mary and her escort arrived late at their next destination. The weather would have made travelling conditions very difficult in the area of heavy clay soil to the south-east of Leicester - the direction of Fotheringhay - and coaches and baggage carts were even more likely than usual to become stuck in mud! 19th-century local historians are probably right in their explanation that the '2 nights watchinge' of the carriages referred to the sensible precaution of leaving the bulky baggage carts behind till the 25th, while Mary was moved on as speedily as the ground conditions allowed.

After leaving Leicester by the East Gate she proceeded along a road with the doom-laden name of Gallowtreegate, which still exists in the city centre. In Tudor times, however, it extended for about three-quarters of a mile from the town walls and joined a Roman road called the Gartree Road. Mary, still travelling backwards, would have had a very clear view of the gallows at the junction of Gallowtreegate with the Gartree Road, when her coach turned onto this. She would never again see any towns. For the rest of the thirty miles or so to Fotheringhay, she travelled through or near many villages which had long been deserted, and others which still had a small population. Such places were owned either by local gentry escorting Mary, or else were royal manors belonging to Elizabeth.

The Gartree Road provided a direct route all the way across to Corby in Northamptonshire, only a short distance from Oundle, the town nearest to Fotheringhay. But it was a lowland road through what a later traveller described as 'the dirty, clayey part of England' and it had the disadvantage of many streams to be crossed. About five miles from Leicester therefore, Mary was jolted onto an ancient ridgeway route which led eventually to the hilly and isolated country along the county boundary between Leicestershire and Rutland. This phase of her final journey began at a deserted village called Great Stretton, one of the manors owned by an influential local family, the Herricks, who were also closely associated with the next village, Houghton-on-the-Hill.

Mary would not have seen the land rising steadily but relentlessly beyond Houghton, yet surely she must have noticed the uncomfortable lurching of her coach as the horses struggled to pull it uphill. And no doubt she continued to ask the coachman about the scenes in front of the coach. If her jailers had deemed it necessary to break the journey because of the bad weather, there were several suitable safe houses along the route which could potentially have been used. A cluster of five deserted medieval villages near Houghton, for instance, had retained their manor houses and were owned by only two families, the Caves and Ashbys, some of whom were amongst Mary's escort through Leicestershire. Other possible stopping-places were at Tilton-on-the-Hill with the Digby family, or their near neighbours, the Tamworths in the adjoining hamlet of Halstead.

A few miles further on was the county boundary, where the escort duties of the Leicestershire gentry ceased and members of the Rutland gentry took over responsibility for guarding and guiding the Queen of Scots through their county. 'A faire house' called Withcote Hall stood near its deserted village, only just inside Leicestershire and also conveniently on the ridgeway between the rivers Gwash and Chater. The dubious honour of playing hosts to Mary for the night before she reached Fotheringhay therefore fell on the Smith family of Withcote. They were first cousins and long-term friends of the Cave family, and the fine early 16th-century chapel near their home still remains in its very rural setting. Mary is unlikely to have appreciated its beauty, though, after such a wet and tiring journey to reach Withcote. A chapel wall plaque commemorating one of the Smiths might have seemed to her like another portent of her fate, if she had been aware of this memorial - it is engraved with the words, 'Lyve to dye and dye to lyve', which is curiously reminiscent of her personal motto, 'In my end is my beginning'.

Surrounded by her enemies, Mary may have been sensitive to feelings of her past preying on her thoughts, in addition to her fears for the future. The Smiths' neighbour and friend at Launde Abbey, a mile from Withcote, certainly had tenuous links with her early and later years. Lord Henry Cromwell was married to Lady Mary Paulet, a kinswoman of Mary's custodian, and through his mother, Elizabeth Seymour, he had close family connections with both the Tudors and the Seymours. For instance, his first cousin King Edward VI had been the husband intended for the Queen of Scots by the English, and another first cousin and childhood friend was the Earl of Hertford, husband of her rival claimant to the throne, Lady Catherine Grey.

Sunday 25th September was the last day of Mary's journey. The remote ridgeway route across the western half of Rutland was through a royal hunting forest called Leighfield and passed by the county town of Oakham two or three miles to the north. Nowadays it is still a lonely way along bridle paths, despite being close to the major tourist attraction of Rutland Water. The deserted village of Martinsthorpe is near the eastern end of the bridle way, shortly before Mary's route joins the modern road along the southern shore of Rutland Water through the villages of Manton and Edith Weston (named after the 11th-century King Edward the Confessor's wife, Queen Edith, who owned the western part of Rutland!).

Elizabeth had granted the manor of Edith Weston to William Parr, Marquess of Northampton, the brother of Queen Katherine Parr. One of the royal emissaries who had conducted Mary to Tixall Hall the previous month was Sir Thomas Gorges, who was now married to William Parr's Swedish-born widow, Helena. She was a friend and favourite of Elizabeth, and also one of the leading ladies in England, with her title of Marchioness - or "the Lady

Marquess" as Elizabeth affectionately called her. Although Helena did not gain possession of Edith Weston when her first husband died, she later received from Elizabeth some property forfeited by conspirators to free Mary Queen of Scots. The personal connections and loyalties of Thomas Gorges predisposed him to being one of the greatest enemies accompanying Mary on the whole of her final journey.

Bourgoing's diary mentioned that they went through Collyweston, where there was a royal palace owned by Elizabeth - another potential safe house in case of any need to bring the journey to a halt. To reach there, the route took Mary south from Edith Weston across the river Chater, near the church at Ketton, a manor which belonged to the Harrington family, who had provided the Sheriff of Rutland for that year.

At Collyweston Bridge the escort duties of the Rutland gentry ended and Mary crossed over the river Welland into Northamptonshire, soon to be the county of her death. She did not fully realize this on entering Northamptonshire, but thoughts may well have occurred to her of the dreadful irony of her situation. As her coach lurched up the steep hill past Collyweston Church, she would have had a good view of the Tudor palace on the level ground at the bottom. Long before, it had been the main residence of her ancestress, Lady Margaret Beaufort, and here Mary's English grandmother, Margaret Tudor, had bidden a tearful farewell to her family on her way north to marry King James IV of Scotland. This union had been expected to bring peace between the English and Scots, but it had left a legacy of bitter resentment and distrust of Mary by Elizabeth, because of Mary's strong claim to the English throne.

Nothing now remains either of Collyweston Palace or Mary's destination at Fotheringhay Castle. The seven miles between these two places were partly through another royal forest, Rockingham, and afterwards through three mellow-stone villages. The middle of these was

Apethorpe, the home of the medical lady, Grace Mildmay. Grace's father-in-law, Sir Walter Mildmay, was a member of Elizabeth's Privy Council, and both he and her husband Anthony travelled with the Queen of Scots all the way from Chartley to Fotheringhay. If Mary had been sent to life imprisonment rather than execution at Fotheringhay Castle, perhaps Bourgoing would have sought Grace's advice about obtaining the herbs he needed in treating his royal mistress.

Beyond the next village of Woodnewton and just outside Fotheringhay, the route joined a road from nearby Oundle called Perio Lane. On hearing this name, Mary is said to have expressed her anguish with a pun on its Latin meaning, "Perio, I perish!" She could not yet see her last earthly home, perched on its steep castle mound, though if she had been facing forward in her coach, she would not have been spared the sight of the royal fortress at Fotheringhay looming ever nearer. After its gates closed behind her, William Cecil, now Lord Burghley, referred to Mary in derogatory terms as the 'Queen of the Castle'.

Mary Queen of Scots blessing her ladies on the scaffold

The accounts of Mary's trial in October 1586, her execution on 8th February 1587 and her great dignity during her remaining months have been numerous. A chair adorned with carvings of angels and one of the Virgin Mary as Queen of Heaven is reputed to have been used by Mary Queen of Scots while the death warrant was read out as she awaited execution. When Fotheringhay Castle was demolished in the 17th century, this time-worn chair was moved to Conington Church in Cambridgeshire by Sir Robert Bruce Cotton. He may well have been influenced long before this by hearing of Mary's final journey, for his stepmother, Dorothy Tamworth, came from Halstead House, near Withcote Hall.

Mary's spirit is said to haunt the Talbot Hotel at Oundle, particularly around each year's anniversary of her death. Some parts of Fotheringhay Castle were built into the structure of this ancient inn, including stonework, a large window the Queen of Scots looked through on that fateful February day and an oak staircase which she may have walked down to her execution - leaving a mark with her ring as she stopped hesitantly at the top of this.

Being accused of seeking Elizabeth's death cost Mary Queen of Scots her own life. Yet the Virgin Queen was not above hoping that Mary's custodian, Paulet, would despatch the captive Queen by private means such as poisoning. Elizabeth berated him for being 'a dainty fellow' when he refused. The execution of a crowned and anointed monarch had hitherto seemed unthinkable, and Elizabeth was well aware that beheading a former reigning Queen of Scotland established an ominous precedent for the future. The manner of Mary's death distressed Elizabeth for sixteen years, until her own departure from this life ended the Tudor Age four centuries ago.

Mary Queen of Scots Chair, Conington Church, Cambridgeshire

Bibliography

Arber, E. (ed.) *A Transcript of the Register of the Company of Stationers of London, 1554-1640, 5 vols. (1894)*

Calendar of Salisbury Manuscripts, Vol.I (1883), Vol.V (1894)

Calendar of State Papers, Domestic, Elizabeth, Addenda,1566-79 (1871)

Caraman, Philip (ed.) *John Gerard, the Autobiography of an Elizabethan* (1951)

Childs, Joy. *A History of Derbyshire* (1987)

Clarke, D.A. (ed.) *Foxe's Book of Martyrs* (1888)

Cox, J.C. *Parish Registers of England* (1910)

Cunningham, Allan. *Traditional Tales of the English and Scottish Peasantry* (1822)

Fletcher, Anthony. *Tudor Rebellions* (3rd edn. 1983)

Foss, Michael. *Tudor Portraits* (1973)

Fox, Evelyn, 'Diary of an Elizabethan Gentlewoman', *Transactions of the Royal Historical Society,* 3rd series, Vol.II (1908)

Hodges, J.P. *The Nature of the Lion* (1962)

Kelly, William. *Royal Progresses and Visits to Leicester* (1884)

Martienssen, Anthony. *Queen Katherine Parr* (1973)

Meadows, Denis. *Elizabethan Quintet* (1956)

Meads, Dorothy M. (ed.) *Diary of Lady Margaret Hoby* (1930)

Parbury, Kathleen. *Women of Grace* (1985)

Plowden, Alison. *Tudor Women* (1979)

Pollock, Linda. *With Faith and Physic, the Life of a Tudor Gentlewoman* (1993)

Prior, Mary (ed.) *Women in English Society, 1500-1800* (1985)

Rowse, A.L. *Simon Forman* (1974)

Salgado, Gamini. *The Elizabethan Underworld* (1977)

Sisson, C.J. *The Judicious Marriage of Mr Hooker* (1940)

Strickland, Agnes. *Lives of the Tudor Princesses* (1868)

Travitsky, Betty. *The Paradise of Women* (1989)

Weigall, Rachel. *'An Elizabethan Gentlewoman', Quarterly Review, No.428* (1911)

White, F.O. *Lives of the Elizabethan Bishops* (1898)

Wilson, Violet. *Queen Elizabeth's Maids of Honour* (1922)

Winchester, Barbara. *Tudor Family Portrait* (1955)

Also by **Marie Sandeford**

The companion volume to
TALES OF TUDOR WOMEN

LONG-LIVED LADIES AND MORE TUDOR TALES

The sixteenth century was said to have had more great women
than any other age of history. Many women made their mark
by surviving to reach their three score years and ten, and beyond,
in the turbulent Tudor world.

Amongst them were 'a woman of masculine understanding' and a
'She-Wolf', a lady who gave her name to a long-distance walk and
another who gave hers to a moth. In this companion volume to
Tales of Tudor Women, long-lived ladies mingle with mysteries,
romances and hauntings, as well as houses of worthy and naughty nuns ...

ISBN 9780953458424   Paperback   160 pages   36 illustrations

Published by Joroby Books, 15 Bridgewater Drive,
                    Great Glen, Leics. LE8 9DX

Long-Lived Ladies and More Tudor Tales can be ordered through U.K. bookshops,
or direct from the publisher at the above address, price £7.50 plus post & packing.

Also by **Marie Sandeford**

THE SECOND SISTER
A Royal Tudor Romance

A story of love, betrayal and intrigue set in the ever-popular Tudor period.

Lady Catherine Grey was the younger sister of Lady Jane, the Nine-Days' Queen of England. After the tragedy of Jane's execution, Catherine sought to rebuild her life through a love-match with the handsome young Edward Seymour and happiness with him at his Wiltshire home.

But her nearness to the throne of Mary Tudor and then Elizabeth, brought her into sharp conflict with her hopes, made her the main rival of Mary Queen of Scots in the line of succession and caused Catherine's love story to become one of unusual devotion ...

'admirably clear on the ongoing struggle for supremacy between the Dudleys, Seymours and Greys ... and catches contemporary anxieties over Elizabeth's continued virginity and the succession'.

Historical Novel Society

'a compelling mixture of history and romantic writing, plus a touch of the thriller'.

Derby Evening Telegraph

ISBN 0 9534584 0 7   Paperback   304 pages   8 illustrations

Published by Joroby Books, 15 Bridgewater Drive,
                Great Glen, Leics. LE8 9DX

The Second Sister can be ordered through U.K. bookshops, or direct from the publisher at the above address, price £8.95 plus post & packing.